Retire
Fit, Fit & Fit

Become Financially, Physically and Emotionally Fit

Howard Pell

Illustrations by Mackenzie Boyd; front cover photograph by Rosemary Pell; back cover photograph by Patrica Dimeck.

Printed in Canada

ISBN 978-0-9950431-0-7

FIN 04 07 2016

Library and Archives Canada Cataloguing in Publication

Pell, Howard Lorne, 1953-, author
Retire fit, fit & fit : become financially, physically and emotionally fit / Howard Pell.

ISBN 978-0-9950431-0-7 (paperback)

1. Retirement. 2. Retirement--Planning. 3. Retirement--Economic aspects. 4. Retirement--Psychological aspects. I. Title.

HQ1062.P445 2016 646.7'9 C2016-902275-7

Contents

Dedication

It is said that the famous British writer Dr. Samuel Johnson was asked by an aspiring author to give his opinion of a new work she had just written. She also asked Dr. Johnson, that if her book wasn't up to par, please tell her, for she had other *irons in the fire*. "In that case," replied the doctor, having read a few pages, "I advise you to put it where your other irons are." This particular iron didn't go with my others primarily because of the huge encouragement of friends and family.

This book is dedicated to the four women who helped to get me Fit, Fit and Fit for my retirement:

My financial advisors, Linda and Kim — who worked very hard in getting us financially fit and on track for a retirement with few, if any, financial worries.

My fitness coach, Missy — who, while working very hard in getting us physically fit and keeping us physically fit whether it was by pushups or squats, always demanded "TWO MORE!"

Most importantly my wife, Rose — who has supported and encouraged me in writing this book and in all my endeavours over the past 40 years.

What a fortunate man I am, to have all these very special women in my life.

Acknowledgements:

I read somewhere that a man just hung and an author just having published a book are nearly in the same predicament — both are in suspense; however, the former is sure to be cut down, while the latter will most certainly be cut up. Although many people helped with this book, any faults you find, hang with me.

No author of a book of this kind creates the book by himself. I can't recall all the many people who gave me a word, a phrase, an idea, that I've incorporated into this book, but you know who you are and I thank you. Of course there were those who went above and beyond and took the time and made the effort to help, read, and comment on what I wrote and I thank them here for that time and effort.

Those who read the early drafts and helped me kill my rants and tone down my weird sense of humour: Marilyn Book, Maureen Crawford, Louise Gardiner, Missy Gore, Diana Jewer, Mary Moore, Maureen Nummelin, Anne Wilbee and Charlene Zietsma. Hmm. As I write this I realize that they are all women — what a lucky guy I am.

To those that read the final drafts again and again: Julie Ashley, Marilyn Book, Louise Gardiner, Missy Gore, Maureen Nummelin, Anne Wilbee and Charlene Zietsma. What troupers you are. A special thank you to Marie Lindsay for her detailed and precise editing skills.

And of course, my wife Rose, who read every draft, helped me with the worksheets and summaries and supported me through it all.

Disclaimers:

I am not a lawyer, but I know enough to ask a lawyer's advice. I am not a financial advisor, but I know enough to ask a financial advisor's advice. I am not an accountant, nor am I a nutritionist, and heaven knows I am not a personal fitness coach. There are many experts in the retirement field, and I am not one of them — I'm just a regular guy who retired. However, having just been through the transition from working to playing, and with the experience still fresh in my mind, I wrote this book with the hope that it will give you the background you need for a successful transition into this new phase of your life.

It should go without saying, but I'll say it anyway: Everything in this book is my opinion. It has been my journey, and I'm sharing what's worked for me and what hasn't. I hope you learn from it and that you find it useful.

Further disclaimer: I mention a lot of products and services in this book, and none of them have paid me for mentioning them. If I like them, it is because I like them. If I don't like them, it is because I don't like them. I just wanted you to know. Their names may be registered trademarks, and you know which ones they are without me telling you.

CHAPTER ONE

The Three Fitnesses

Is This Book For You?

It seems that our society has become so fragmented these days that every little difference is yet another demographic. Every demographic has its own champions and detractors, its own TV show and even its own magazine.

While I wrote this book primarily for those who are on the threshold of retirement, I think that young adults will also benefit from reading this book, as starting the process when you are young and developing your three fitnesses early will help you maintain those fitnesses as you get closer to your retirement. I think this book may also be useful to those people who have already retired but who are finding that retirement really isn't what they thought it would be or what they wanted it to be. I hope those people find this book helpful in diagnosing where their expectations for their retirement differ from the reality and assists them to develop a plan to either change their expectations or change the reality.

I'm also hoping that this book will be useful to financial and retirement advisors as another resource to help your clients. And of course, those people with parents, or friends who aren't facing the reality of planning for their retirement. Please use this book to help them along.

And then one day you find, ten years have got behind you
No one told you when to run, you missed the starting gun

Pink Floyd

But the primary audience for this book are those adults in their 40s, 50s and possibly even in their early 60s who are just starting to think about their retirement. If you are in your 60s and are just thinking of retiring now, you may have a bit more difficulty getting Fit, Fit, Fit, but as they say, "It's never too late to begin." If you're in your 40s or 50s, then now is the time to get yourself Fit, Fit, Fit for your retirement. Don't think if you ignore your retirement it will go away, or that you'll deal with it later. You already know how the time slips away. Don't wait another day; read this book and get to it.

I really don't recall when retirement as an entity became such a big thing in Canada; certainly nobody mentioned it to me when I was growing up. And it wasn't even on my radar until I was well into my 30s. Even then all they told me was I needed to start my Registered Retirement Savings Plans (RRSPs), because the two big scares were that (1) we were heading for another Ice-Age so I needed to keep warm in my retirement, and (2) that the Canada Pension Plan (CPP) fund would run out of money by the time I retired. Looks like they were wrong on both accounts. My wife and I were probably like many young Canadians who were totally unprepared and uneducated for our own retirement. The school system never mentioned it, our parents never mentioned it, and even the dude who sold us our first mutual funds for our first RRSP never told us. Now it seems to be on everyone's lips, in all the papers and magazines. It is certainly in all the banks and on billboards. And I think that is a good thing. In fact, I'm still hopeful that one of these days the public schools might even begin teaching students, all students, about banking, budgeting, loans and even preparing for retirement.

(For my USA readers, look for your flag to see the USA equivalents)
The American equivalent of a
Canadian RRSP (Registered Retirement Savings Plan) is a 401(k)
CPP (Canada Pension Plan) = American Old Age Pension

So if you're seriously thinking about your retirement or are just curious about it, and you have a few years before that happens, then this book is for you. If you still have more than a decade until you retire, please don't put it off, thinking, "Oh well, I have years yet, so there is no hurry." Regardless of how much time you have until your retirement, don't forget what the guy who writes fortune cookie fortunes once said, "The best day to plant a tree was 20 years ago, the second-best day is today."

Our time on this earth is finite, and it's always shorter than we think. How do we want to spend it? Will we give of ourselves to others, so that the world will be richer because we passed through it? Or will we spend our days, as the famous Indian poet Rabindranath Tagore wrote, in stringing and unstringing our instruments, while the song we came to sing remains unsung?

K.R. Ravindran,
2015-16 President Rotary International

What Is This Book About?

Another retirement self-help book?

Yes, another retirement self-help book. Having read many retirement self-help books in the run-up to my own recent retirement, I felt there was a need to net it all out and bring it all together in one place and to eliminate what I considered dross. There were too many books that felt like they were written by experts using their technical knowledge but not their first-hand experiential knowledge. So I decided to put it all together in one volume; only the good stuff, only the stuff you need to prepare yourself. Here are my thoughts on retirement based on my own experience.

retirement |ri'tīrmənt|
Noun

Clearly, it means different things to different people. For me, it means: doing what I want without having to ask to be paid for doing it ... well, mostly. Like the characters in Downton Abbey who primarily live off the interest and principal of their fabulous fortunes, my wife and I will live off what we've managed to squirrel away (plus whatever CPP brings us).

For you it may mean something similar, or it may mean working part-time doing something you've never done before. It may mean a whole new career in a whole new field. It may mean returning to school to complete your undergraduate or get that Masters degree you always wanted. Perhaps you want to apply for a research grant to find out The Effect of Country Music on Suicide.[1] Yup, someone

[1] www.jstor.org/stable/579974?seq=1#page_scan_tab_contents

actually got funding to find out if listening to country music caused people to kill themselves.

There are many, many things you must consider before your retirement: where you live, who you live with, your lifestyle, your hobbies, the list goes on. All of these are important; however, I believe they can be summarized by what, in my opinion and experience, are the three most important issues:

- Financial Fitness,
- Physical Fitness, and
- Emotional Fitness.

Without all three of these fitnesses, all your other decisions lose their relevance.

Please Don't Panic

Okay, so perhaps you are not Fit, Fit, Fit today. You may even think it impossible to get Fit, Fit, Fit by the time you'd like to retire. Well, don't panic. In this book, I offer many ideas on how to get you close, if not all the way to your fitness goals. Or, if we can't get you Fit, Fit, Fit enough for your retirement goals, then we'll look at modifying your goals.

Of course, some of the people reading this book are fit in one or two of these three fitnesses already. Perhaps you are financially fit as well as physically fit; Great! Or you are physically fit and emotionally fit;

Terrific! But I suspect that most of you could benefit from increasing your fitness in one, two or all three of these areas.

As the title of this book suggests, I want to encourage you to be fit for retirement in these three broad categories: financial, physical and emotional. With one or two of these three you can certainly retire; however, as I'll explain, to retire well I believe you must be fit in all three. Let's look at the diagram below. There are the three areas of fitness I've mentioned, and right in the centre where they intersect is the sweet spot. And of course we want to make that sweet spot as large as possible.

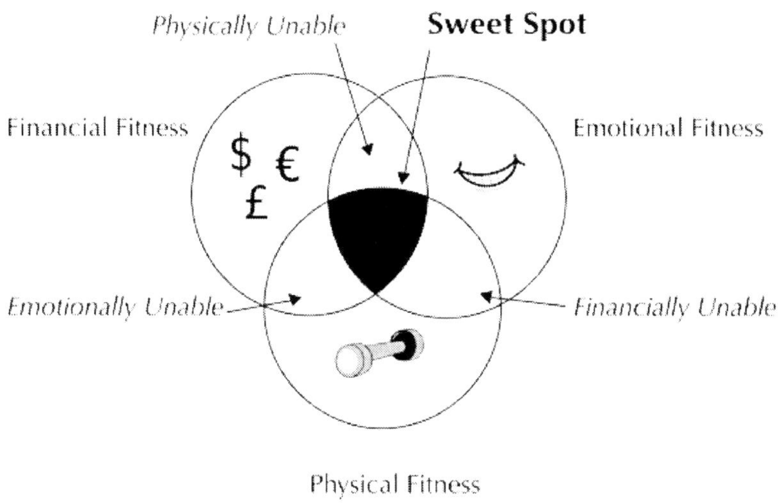

Figure 1: The Three Fitnesses

But what if you are missing any one or two of these fitnesses?

1. You are only Financially Fit

If you are financially fit but you acquired that fitness by selling your physical and/or emotional health, you can financially afford to retire but without your physical health you won't be moving around very much, and as any moving around will be done without very much motivation because of your lack of emotional fitness, you may just end up sitting in front of your TV for the next 20 years. Or quite possibly it will only buy you 5 years or 10 years of retirement instead of the 20 or 30 you hoped for because of your poor physical or emotional health. Truly a sad way to live out the rest of your life.

2. You are only Physically Fit

If you are physically fit but don't have the financial resources and are not emotionally prepared, then you might not be able to pay the rent and put food on the table if you stop working, and even if you somehow were able to quit work, you won't have the motivation — emotional fitness — to do anything with your free time. So you'll be physically healthy, but will need to keep working even if you are ready to stop: surely a frustrating way to cap off your life.

3. You are only Emotionally Fit

If you are emotionally ready but lack the finances and the physical health to retire you may be in the worst position of all. You have all sorts of things you want to get involved with and you are just itching to get to them, but without your health and without the finances those things may stay just out of your reach.

Meeting Your Needs

As I previously mentioned, there are many other factors that will be more or less important to you as you consider your retirement, each of us is different and has different needs and wants. Things important to me may be completely irrelevant to you. For example,

I'm a city boy; but perhaps a small town suits you best. I'm a cat person but you can't wait to retire to buy that St. Bernard puppy you've always wanted. You need a garden to putter in while I prefer to do my puttering on 18 holes. I like to tie flies, you like to tie one on. Even so, these three categories: financial, physical and emotional fitness are critical to all of us and it is these three areas of fitness that I explore in this book.

As I mentioned, many retirement books focus on your financial fitness and completely ignore the other two. We are complex beings and have a range of needs beyond financial. Tony Robbins, in *Why We Do What We Do,* identifies Six Human Needs.[2] I believe that concentrating on all three Fitnesses will apply to meet these six needs.

1. **Certainty**: assurance you can avoid pain and gain pleasure
2. **Uncertainty/Variety**: the need for the unknown, change, new stimuli
3. **Significance**: feeling unique, important, special or needed
4. **Connection/Love**: a strong feeling of closeness or union with someone or something
5. **Growth**: an expansion of capacity, capability or understanding
6. **Contribution**: a sense of service and focus on helping, giving to and supporting others.

The first of the six needs, "Certainty", is really the only one, in my opinion, that can be addressed by financial fitness. Yes, you also need physical fitness for it as well, but being physically fit doesn't guarantee you can afford to purchase those things that help you avoid pain and gain pleasure. And to attain the fifth need "Growth" it certainly helps to have money, but all the other human needs seem to fall under the category of emotional fitness and we'll look at them in the chapter on emotional fitness.

---

[2] training.tonyrobbins.com/the-6-human-needs-why-we-do-what-we-do/

Sounds Like a Plan

If you're reading this, it means you're either thinking about, or are intrigued by, the idea of retiring. Now you're ready to plan for this exciting period of your life. Planning is the key to achieving anything. You know you'll need to finance your retirement, so you know you'll need a financial plan. This book will help you create one. But your retirement plan is much, much more than the financial plan alone. You may not have a clear idea of what physical activities you'll do in your retirement, but you know you'll need to be physically fit to do them, so you'll need a plan to get physically fit too. Again, this book will help you create one. And in the same way, you'll want to get emotionally fit to enjoy your retirement, and again, you'll need a plan. This book will help you do that too. Please turn to Appendix A and photocopy the plan. Then as you read through the book you can update your plan.

As you move towards retirement, keep thinking about tweaking your plans to give you direction to be Fit, Fit and Fit for those retirement years.

Three Phases of Retirement

The way I see it, there are really three phases of retirement: "Fit", "Contentment" and "Geezer".

1. The first phase is your *Fit* phase. You are healthy, strong, alert. You are raring to go and you are ready to do things, go places and meet people. Look out world, I'm newly-retired and I'm gonna enjoy myself like I never did while I was working. Damn the torpedoes, full speed ahead.

2. The second phase is the *Contentment* phase. You are still healthy, strong and alert but now your desire and/or energy is waning. Rather than the thrills and excitement of travel and other active pursuits, you'd rather spend your time enjoying your community, family and your home. Perhaps it is time for more relaxing hobbies, spending more time with your grandchildren, that sort of thing.

3. I call the final phase the *Geezer* phase. Your health is failing, your memory and cognitive powers are failing. You stumble more, perhaps you need a walker or wheelchair. Your days consist of eating, sleeping and pooping, and not much more (hmmm, sounds like your old St. Bernard).

As someone approaching retirement, you probably know people in all three phases, perhaps even your parents or in-laws. My goal, and I suspect your goal too, is to maximize the Fit and Contentment phases and minimize the Geezer phase.

Just a brief word about my retirement before we go on. I had a great position with a great company. I was coming up to my 20th anniversary with them and to my 60th birthday. I could have stayed on for another 20 years if I wanted; I'm sure they would have had me. Only one thing troubled me, death. Not really my death, but my friends, spouses of friends and associates' deaths; they were dying.

They had plans, dreams of years of retirement, travel, hobbies, living their golden years; and they died far too young. They were my age, some a bit younger, some a bit older, but my age and they were gone. I took a hard look at my life and asked myself what was more important; more money from my job or more time. Time to spend with my wife, my family, my friends. Time to do the things I really wanted to do. So I chose time, and I have never had a moment of regret for the decision I made.

> As I was working on the final draft of this book, we had just been to two more funerals. The first, a fellow Rotarian, in her mid-40s and in the prime of her life. The second, the partner of one of my wife's best friends, just turned 60. Both died of cancer. It just reinforces that my wife and I made the right decision for me to retire now.

I was relating all this to my 87 year-old father and he reminded me that all his friends are dead. All his high school buddies, work friends, social club friends. All dead — all except for Herbie who moved to Florida, which according to dad is just about the same thing.

I should point out that there was no company pension waiting for me. My employer of 20 years never had a company pension, and probably never will; and my wife is self-employed. This means we have to make do on what we have saved and whatever the Canadian government will pay us when we start collecting our pensions. Because of this, fairly early on in our married life my wife and I decided that while we had to live for today, we also had to make choices that let us save for tomorrow, as no one else was going to do it for us. In those early years we truly knew nothing about saving for our retirement, so we started educating ourselves. Ultimately we found our current financial advisors, and they educated us further, and they continue to educate us now that we are retired and are no longer growing our savings but spending them. We both agree that saving for tomorrow didn't detract from our ability to live for today to any serious extent — you just have to find the right balance. Looking back, we might have missed a few things; but, like Old Blue-Eyes sang about regrets: "I've had a few, but then again too few to mention."

> And while I'm at it, what they say is true, I am far busier now than I ever was when I was working: busier with my wife, my family, my friends and my hobbies. The big difference is that now all my deadlines and commitments are self-imposed. And I'm having a blast! I hope you will too.

Finally, I really think we need a new name for this state of voluntary unemployment I've just entered. The word "retired" just doesn't work for me. When I hear it, I have a mental image of a group of withered, old men sitting at a sidewalk cafe, smoking, drinking espresso and playing dominos. Yes, they're in the Contentment phase all right, but that's not me. Or I think of elderly couples, with walkers shuffling through a city park. That's not me either, and it shouldn't be you when you start this phase. Oddly enough, I don't think of those in the Geezer phase as being retired for some reason. And that's definitely not me — I have many, many years (I hope) until I reach that phase.

So rather than fight the connotation of the word "retired," I think we need a new name. I'm open to suggestions, but it has to invoke the mental image of the following characteristics:

- Virility
- Health
- Mobility
- Curiosity
- Eagerness to learn
- Eagerness to do
- Dream fulfillment
- Play mode

Some suggestions:

- VUP - Voluntarily Unemployed Person
- OOTL (pronounced oo-tel) - Oldies On The Loose
- BTDT (pronounced BeeTee DeeTee) - Been There, Done That

Or perhaps we just adopt the Spanish word for "retired" which is "Jubilado" (male), "Jubilada" (female). Doesn't that sound grand? Just like "jubilation", and some days that's exactly how I feel.

The author's wife in Spain. "Cierre Por Jubilación" = "Closing for Retirement"

In other words, someone who is financially, physically and emotionally fit. If you think of a new word, post it on my blog at www.howardpell.ca or drop me a line at hlpell@howardpell.ca.

A tip of the hat to Julie for pointing out "Who wants the word 'tired' in this station of life?"

Now's the time for you to get Fit, Fit and Fit before your retirement. If you're ready, please read on.

CHAPTER TWO

Financially Fit

Your economic security does not lie in your job; it lies in your own power to produce — to think, to learn, to create, to adapt. That's true financial independence. It's not having wealth; it's having the power to produce wealth. It's intrinsic.

Stephen R. Covey

No one's ever achieved financial fitness with a January resolution that's abandoned by February.

Suze Orman

Financial freedom is a mental, emotional and educational process.

Robert Kiyosaki

Introduction

It seems that almost all retirement books either deal exclusively with the financial aspect of retirement or it is their primary thrust, so I decided to deal with financial fitness first. Without enough money to see you through to the end of time — well, the end of *your* time — you will spend a lot of that time just worrying about money; and what fun is that? Didn't you spend a lot of your youth (and perhaps early married life) worrying about money? And as you recall, that definitely wasn't fun. The key word here is *enough*. What is *enough* money for me might only be a start for you, and vice versa.

There are two primary issues we need to discuss:

1. When is *the end of time* for you, and
2. How much money is *enough*?

There are a number of factors that we'll review to determine the answers to both these questions. We will also talk about planning and the various plans you will make. We will touch on insurance and a few other issues.

We conclude the chapter with a look at getting help from professionals to assist you in making all these plans.

Don't forget to turn to Appendix A and photocopy the plan. Then as you read through the book you can update your plan.

The idea is to die young as late as possible.
Ashley Montagu

When Will You Die?

Interesting question, and, unless you see to it yourself (remember the country music study), impossible to answer with any accuracy. Yet the bulk of your financial planning hinges on your answer to this one question. Whether you wish to die with your last dollar in your pocket, or you subscribe to the adage that "he who dies with the most toys wins," or you prefer something in between these extremes, you can't stop working without knowing how much money you'll need. And you won't know how much money you'll need until you know how long your savings will need to last (at least until the day you die, and longer if you wish to leave some of it to others).

If you happen to be one of the rare people with a good pension, or those even rarer people who have pensions indexed to the cost of living, you can skip the rest of this chapter safe in the knowledge that everyone else reading this book is getting in line for surf and turf on your yacht. The rest of us just have to face the fact that without a comfy pension, we must look after ourselves, and so to the rest of us I say, read on.

"Your Mileage May Vary"

As I write this, Statistics Canada[3] reports that the average life expectancy for Canadians born in the early 1950s is 66 years for men

[3] Statistics Canada - www.statcan.gc.ca/tables-tableaux/sum-som/101/cst01/health26-eng.htm

and 71 years for women. You, Mr. or Ms. Boomer, who is reading this, are way ahead of the game as you have already lived longer than those who reduced the average age by dying young. The Globe and Mail ran a very interesting article[4] in 2014 that indicates that 60-year-olds in 2013 could live another 25 years — our reward for making it this far. You'll find the original Statistics Canada report that this article is based on by following this link.[5] So if you were 60 in 2013, your life expectancy is closer to 85 (for men) than the 66 average.

Okay, this is just a guess on my part but I'm going to say that these numbers should be close for Americans. After all, these are really just averages and "your mileage may vary."

Of course your mileage may vary, but let's see if we can pin it down a bit.

In recent years there has been a proliferation of calculators on the Internet. A web search for "life expectancy calculator Canada" will find lots of these (there is a list of some of them at the end of this chapter). I guarantee that you will get a different number from each of them, so you may want to try a number of these calculators and take an average of the results.

These calculators can only give you a ballpark number, so if one says you will live to 100, but you are run over by a bus next week, don't

---

[4] Globe and Mail - www.theglobeandmail.com/report-on-business/economy/canadian-life-expectancy-gains-expected-to-slow/article18031842/

[5] Statistics Canada - www.osfi-bsif.gc.ca/Eng/oca-bac/as-ea/Pages/mpsspc.aspx

expect to sue them with any success. Besides, most lawyers insist on their clients having warm bodies.

Trying different inputs to these calculators can be fun and enlightening, and I encourage you to play with them. Also look at what the calculators are telling you about how a change in your lifestyle today could lengthen (or shorten) your life expectancy. You may also want to factor in other information not asked for by these calculators, factors that might seriously shorten your life expectancy: things like family history of genetic illnesses or diseases or the fact that you engage in dangerous hobbies like sky diving, testing aircraft or lion taming. Also consider factors that may lengthen your life: perhaps you've volunteered in a medical or health study; with any luck, you're not in the control group.

So go ahead, try one or two of these calculators. I'll wait.

Okay, you now have a guesstimate of when you will die. Let's take me as an example and the StatsCan report I referenced above. I was 60 in 2013, so I may live another 25 years, so let's say 85. Now subtract my current age (I'm writing this in late 2015 and I'll soon be 62): 85 - 62 = 23. This is how many years I will have to support myself if I retired today. After this calculation, multiply this number of years (23) by my current salary to get a rough idea of how much money I'll need.

You try it:

A	Your Life Expectancy Guesstimate	Years
B	Your Retirement Age	Years
C	Subtract (A - B) — This is the number of years you'll live without working	Years
D	Your Current Salary	$
E	Multiply (C * D) — This is how much you'll need to save.	$

YIPES! Okay, so you won't be telling your boss what to do with your job just yet.

That last calculation (E) about how much money you'll need wasn't exactly true as it doesn't take into account that some of your current salary goes into savings, which it won't once you retire. It also doesn't include: inflation, income from government sources, or the general growth in your savings each year. It is a bit more complicated than that, and sorting this out is the goal of the rest of this chapter.

How Long Will My Money Last?

When I was just out of high school and bouncing from job to job and trying to figure out what I wanted to do with my life, I got caught by an unexpected (to me) layoff. It was then that one of my soon-to-be-ex co-workers who was considerably older than me gave me some startling advice. He said:

"You should always keep about a month's salary in the bank for when you are between jobs."

Biff! Pow! Holy bank account Batman, I had never heard this before, and all of a sudden it made infinite sense. But somehow it also dawned on me: Why stop at a month's salary? Why not 2 months or 12 months? And the more I thought of this, the more this bit of advice, coupled with the scare story that the Canadian government wouldn't have any money for my pension by the time I needed it, really began to motivate me to save. It was some years later that I heard this next incentive (as if I really needed one by then):

"The rich plan for three generations;
the poor plan for Saturday night."

I just love this quote, attributed to Gloria Steinem. Go on, read it again, it's worth it. As I had no desire to have children, the three generations thing was out, but the gist of the message was not lost on me. So where does that leave us? It boils down to how much you have already saved and how much you can squirrel away before you stop working.

Okay, ready? We can do some simple calculations to see how long your money will last (at least until you die, we hope). Again, there are lots of calculators on the web you can use. Try your bank's or financial planner's web site (see the end of this chapter for some references). There are also calculator spreadsheets available for Numbers, Libre Office, Open Office and Excel. All these calculators are based on some assumptions you need to make.

Honestly, I was going to walk you through a web calculator here but of course I can't guarantee that the calculator will still be there by the time you read this, and if it is there, I can't guarantee that it won't have changed. So rather than a screen shot of a calculator (and risk copyright infringement) I'm going to cover the typical inputs that most calculators require. May I suggest you read this next part (even read it a couple of times) and then find a calculator you like (again, see the references at the end of the chapter) work through this section and do the calculator at the same time.

Here is what you're going to need to know:

1. Your post-retirement income requirement
2. Inflation rate
3. Rate of return on your savings

1. **Post-retirement income** — everyone, and it seems like absolutely everyone, has an opinion on how much you'll need to retire as a percentage of your current salary and these vary wildly. Many of these sound quite reasonable, but which one do you go with? Did you hear the one about the two economists? Put them in a room together, and they'll come up with three opinions. Yes I know, sorry. The point remains that without a financial advisor who takes the time to learn about you and your circumstances, one person's opinion is just as valid as the next. But will it be right for you? See my section below on advisors.

   My suggestion is that you be generous here. If you think you will maintain roughly the same lifestyle, same spending habits, same number of trips, same hobbies, etc. once you retire, then perhaps you will need roughly the same income less the amount you're now saving for these happy years. If you plan on doing more, top-drawer, travel you may need more income. And if you plan on spending your golden years doing nothing more than whiling away your days in your greenhouse developing the perfect black rose, perhaps you can get by on a lot less.

How do you know what will work for you? Consider this: If you are within a few years of retirement, start living on the income level you think you'll be able to live on when you stop working. Track your expenses every month and get a feel for it. Have you overestimated? Have you underestimated? Keep adjusting until you find the Goldilocks balance, just right. If it sounds like too much work tracking your expenses, stop using cash. Only use your debit and credit cards, and it is all tracked for you. Or set up a system where you "pay" yourself just part of each paycheque, with the rest of your salary deposited to one of your accounts and see where you stand at the end of the month. Are you a bit short? Do you have a lot left over? The point is, can you live on the amount you have set as a goal for your retirement? If not, you need to rethink a few things. Ask your financial advisor, banker or accountant to help you with this. They will be happy to assist.

2. **Inflation rate/cost of living during your retirement** — this is just a guess. Search for the current inflation rate on the Internet and plug it in to the calculator. Will the inflation rate go up or will it go down before you die? Yes it will. A lot of people get paid a lot of money to make predictions (read: guesses) about this. Some of them are actually right some of the time. Your

guess will be just as good as most of the experts; after all, if they really could predict the inflation rate, interest rate, exchange rates, we'd be the absolute last people in the world they would tell. Historical data can be interesting, but as everyone is wont to say, it is no predictor; however, just for kicks, check out this interesting Canadian Inflation Calculator.[6]

3. **Rate of return on your savings** — this is much more complicated. Your savings will be invested in a mix of investments, so you need to find the average return you expect to get. What have you been getting for the past couple of years? Do you think you can maintain that? Improve on that? Plug in a number that you think is attainable. Will interest rates go up or will they go down before you die? Yes they will. Again, a lot of people get paid a lot of money to make predictions, and again, some of them are right some of the time. Go on, take a guess. But try to make it a reasonable guess; if the banks are paying 1% for GICs and last year your investments made 10%, it probably isn't realistic to expect your investments to return 20% each year from here on. Obviously, you want to err on the side of caution here so you can be pleasantly surprised when your investments do better than you predicted.

GIC (Guaranteed Investment Certificate)
= Term Deposit or Fixed Annuity

[6] inflationcalculator.ca/

Well that's it. What did the calculator say? You need $1 million? $3 million? $500,000? Do you have it, or will you have it when you retire through a combination of savings assets, private pension and government pension? Yes? Fantastic! No? Time to make some choices.

The Canada Pension Plan — Where do I even begin? This is such a complex topic, I'm going to leave it for you to discuss with your Financial Advisor. The whole notion of when to start taking it is a gamble, with the government as the dealer. There are many stories of those who start collecting early and live to a ripe old age with the minimum paid each month. Then there are the stories of those who start collecting later to get a larger monthly payment and pass away two months later. Talk with your advisor.

"You Can't Always Get What You Want"

If you are short of your financial goals, there are many things you can do so you can still retire. Here are a few options to think about.

- **Retire later** — Do you remember "Freedom-55"? Of course you do.

Hmm, perhaps you don't remember, it was an advertising campaign by London Life Insurance Co. telling us how they were going to help us all retire at age 55.

Well, did you achieve it? If you're reading this book then I'll assume you didn't — I certainly didn't. Re-run the calculator with a later date of retirement. Does an extra year or two of working and saving make enough of a difference? For me it was Freedom-60; those 5 extra years really made a difference. You work longer, invest more and save more, and your investments grow more (we hope — remember 2008). Everyone will tell you to start saving early in life because compound interest is your friend. A few more years of saving at the end of your working life won't do much for you growth-wise, but postponing dipping into your savings for an additional year or two might help quite a bit. You might even consider taking a part-time job when you retire. This could be with your current company or somewhere else. You get more free time and still get some money coming in, so your savings last a few extra years.

- **Live on less** — Is your expected retirement lifestyle too grand? To retire when you want to, you may have to live a simpler life. We've all read the advice that it is cheaper to live when you retire because you save on business expenses like dry cleaning, etc. Really!? Since "biz-casual" changed into "beachwear" for many office workers, this just doesn't cut it. Some will need more income when they retire, some less and some the same as when they were working. It really boils down to you and what you want to do. If you're like me, and time is more important than money, living on less may be your best bet.

- **Save more** — Have you been putting away the minimum RRSP contribution each year and just living for today? Can you live a bit more frugally now so you can retire sooner? What if I could save you $46,500 in the next 10 years that you could invest for your retirement? Are you interested in saving that kind of money? And that doesn't include interest on your money. Here's how: Do you really need a large double-double or a skinny, frozen, tall mochaccino twice a day? Check out this Coffee Cost Calculator.[7] Are you drinking enough Timmy's to pay for a week for two at an all-inclusive? We'll come back to Tim's later, but consider that 10 years of two Tim's coffees a day will cost you around $1,000 every year, which is $10,000 in 10 years. Brewing your own at $0.25 each will cost less than $65 a year.

- **Stop Smoking** — Are you still smoking? Check out this Smoking Cost Calculator.[8] A pack a day at 10 bucks each will set you back $36,500 every 10 years! I quit smoking in 1997, and the calculator shows I have saved $65,700! And that doesn't include interest on investing that money. So in the next 10 years you can save $10,000 in coffee and $36,500 in smokes for a grand total of $46,500. For that kind of money, I'll bet you quit smoking today **and** you'll stop at Canadian Tire on the way home and buy a coffee maker so you can start making your own.

Double-double = Two creams, two sugars in your coffee. Also, triple-triple, and (if you can believe it) a 4x4 — so why even put coffee in it?

Timmy's = Tim Hortons, a coffee shop

Canadian Tire = An automotive & department store

[7] Coffee Cost Calculator - www.hughcalc.org/coffee.cgi

[8] Smoking Cost Calculator - https://www.quitnow.ca/tools-and-resources/calculate-your-savings

- **Retire with less** — Do you really need to leave a pot of money to your, or someone else's, kids? I always told my parents and my in-laws that they earned their money so they should enjoy it and not worry about leaving it to me and my siblings. And for the most part my in-laws did spend it and enjoyed it, and we're happy they did. I'm very happy to say that my father is still active at age 87 and is having a great time on my and my sisters' inheritance. Go Dad!

- **Move** — Overheard on the Toronto subway:

    She: You're just building castles in the air.

    He: Where else? We can't afford a building lot here!

    (Pause for riotous laughter).

Do you live in Vancouver or Toronto, Canada's most expensive cities? Many Canadians do. Well, you won't believe this, but millions and millions of Canadians live in smaller communities (and I don't mean Mississauga) and have full, meaningful lives. Crazy, eh? Not only is the pace of life calmer, but it is cheaper too. As I write this, regular gas is selling for $1.19 a litre in Toronto and $1.32 in Vancouver. Around the corner from me in Kitchener it's $1.12, and that's just one example. Check out this Cost Of Living Comparison[9] website for some startling numbers (e.g., Toronto purchasing power is 25.24% lower than Kitchener). Okay, perhaps your job requires you to live in the city, but you can still consider retiring to a smaller town. We have the second largest country in the world and are blessed with some of the most beautiful cities and towns in the world, full of the friendliest, nicest people in the world. Check it out — go for a driving vacation and visit some smaller centres. I'm sure you'll find something you'll like that's more affordable than the city.

[9] www.numbeo.com/cost-of-living/compare_cities.jsp?country1=Canada&country2=Canada&city1=Kitchener&city2=Toronto

Eh? = Huh?

- **Move in with the kids** — Hey! They did it to you, moving home after their attempt at making it on their own. Your turn to move in with them. And after a month or two, get yourself that St. Bernard puppy.

- **Change jobs** — Did you get a whopping 1% salary increase last year? Could you work for the competition and ask for a 10% or 15% increase for moving? Okay, you're reading a retirement book, so you think you're too old to change jobs. Nonsense. As the population ages, your skills and experience are more valuable than ever. (Notice how I didn't disparage today's youth? I hear many stories about entitlement in the latest crop of newly-minted employees; however, I know some truly fine young adults who give me a lot of hope for the future.) Call up a headhunter and see what's out there for you. This also applies to my next point.

- **Change careers** — Are you qualified, or could you get qualified, to get a better paying job or one that has a great pension? How about going into politics? Yeah, politics. Just think: There's no previous experience required, no performance evaluation, a big, fat pay cheque, unlimited expense account (if you don't get caught) and the best, indexed pension in the world. If you have a thick skin and the ability to toe the party line, it's a cinch.

Some Mothers Do 'Ave 'Em

Do you or don't you? Some people were born to have children. A young couple we know have the best children in the world. Their two boys (7 and 11) are polite, inquisitive, bright, creative and inherited the very best of both parents. Ah, if only everyone had children like them. My wife and I, on the other hand, decided early that we weren't parental material and so decided to spare the world from the devil's spawn we were sure we would create. And aren't you happy we decided to stay DINKs (remember Dual Income No Kids)?

Of course if you do decide to 'ave 'em, you will want to decide how many, 1, 2, 3, etc. Some stop at one for various reasons, and some just aren't happy unless there are a dozen of the little darlings running around, to the point that they adopt and foster even more. True heroes! The reason I raise this topic is that if you have children, you probably want to leave some kind of inheritance to them (and/or your grandchildren) when you die.

We'll talk about leaving a legacy to charities later, but for now we'll concentrate on children. So what does it matter if you have children or not? The primary difference for this discussion is this: Will you want to leave any money to your kids? Or, if you are childless like my wife and I, do you want to leave any money to someone else's kids? Your nieces or nephews, or even their kids? This is important. If you don't have kids, or if you do but think they should fend for themselves without your help from beyond the grave, then dying broke is much easier to accomplish than trying to ensure there is something left for your offspring. Come to think of it, if your kids never repaid all the "loans" you gave them over the years, you could turn it around on them and take out a loan yourself. In the

Temptations classic song *Papa was a Rolling Stone,* I never knew if "All he left us was..." Alone, or A Loan.

Can't get that song out of your head now? Sorry about that.

> Speaking about loans to families: Don't. If you want to invest in family members, that's fine. But don't ever expect to get your money back. If the family member does repay you, consider that a bonus. You might even want to "forgive" the repayment, but don't expect it back, and don't count on it towards your retirement. In a nutshell: Risk only what you can afford to lose. Only give money to your family that you can afford to give.

Of course, there are lots of options for disposing of any surplus cash or things you can't take with you (see the section on wills in the Emotionally Fit chapter), but for planning purposes you need to decide on this fundamental thing. And if you decide to leave your, or anyone else's, kids something, then now's the time to decide how much you'd like to leave. This can be calculated in two ways: The first is to consider the lump sum you want to have when you die and the percentage of that lump sum that each of your beneficiaries will get.

Let's say you want to leave a million because you like the sound of it. Also, for all those people who said you'd never amount to anything (like your high school guidance counsellor or your spouse's Aunt Katherine), wouldn't it be nice to rub their noses in it? Let's also say you have ten people on your A-list. So that leaves a hundred grand to each person, right? Wrong. There are fees to be paid: to the lawyers, the executor, the people who will dispose of your assets, and of course the government has its hand out as well. Your lawyer, accountant or financial advisor can give you all the details, but the essence is that you either have to start with more than a million (so you can pay all these extras) or be satisfied with leaving less than this nice-sounding number that you picked out of the air because it sounded good.

Notice that, you do not leave specific dollar amounts because it can get very messy for the lawyers, and lawyers don't like messy things. Suppose your will says you want to leave $1,000 to your firstborn and the remainder to your second. What would happen if your estate only had $900 after all the extras are paid? Your lawyer won't let you do this in your will, so better to think in terms of percentages instead of hard numbers.

The second way is to calculate the percentage for each person first, then decide the amount for the smallest or the largest percentage and then add it up. For example: Let's say you want each of your three children to have an equal share, and it would be nice if they netted out a million each. You'll need to leave $3 million plus the extras already mentioned. But what if you also happen to have a favourite nephew that you'd like to leave a few bucks? Perhaps give your kids 30% each and the remaining 10% to your nephew.

Both methods give you a rough number, and that's all you're really after at this stage. Now your advisors can tell you what your estate will pay in fees and taxes.

I really hope I'm not scaring you with all these millions I'm throwing about. You're saying, "Wait just a doggone minute, I don't have millions, and if I did I might not be leaving any to the kids." More on that later, but the "millions" are just easy things for me to type on my iPad, with a bit of wishful thinking added in. Leaving hundreds or thousands is just the same thing, so please don't let the "millions" put you off.

Notice that we're assuming you keep everything until you die. There is an alternative. Give it away now. In Canada all gifts are tax-free, and this includes gifts of money. I mention this because you might want to sell some of your possessions and give the proceeds to your kids now, or just give them those possessions so they can do what they want with them. That way you can share in their enjoyment of the fruits of your labour. Why not sell your cottage or some stock and take the whole family to an all-inclusive in Cancun for the whole winter? Or buy each of them a St. Bernard puppy.

Where Does The Money Come From?

But wait, there is a fundamental flaw with all these calculators: They make the assumption that if you need $x to live on this year then you will need $x + inflation next year, and the year after that, and the year after that, for the rest of your life. While in the early retirement years, this assumption is mostly valid; however, as we age, many of us will slow down and cut out some activities, especially the more physically demanding ones. You may spend most of your Fit phase travelling the world, but find that when you reach your Contentment phase you would rather read about travel (or write about the travel you did) than actually do it. Perhaps in your 60s you love renovating your home, but perhaps your mobility doesn't allow you to climb ladders and lay flooring in your 70s or 80s. Perhaps you've purchased all the cool fly-fishing feathers and fur to last three lifetimes and enough rods and reels to open your own fishing shop, so now you don't need anything more than the river. (Sigh! Sounds like heaven!) Given this, your expenses may actually decrease.

Of course some of you will point out that as we reach our Geezer phase our health may deteriorate to the point where we need attendant care, meaning our expenses may grow even more than the inflation rate even though we have given up expensive travel. Very true, but we just can't predict this with any kind of accuracy. So I'm suggesting that even though the linear spending model that these calculators use may not be even close to your actual retirement experience, given there is no way to accurately predict your physical fitness or general health in the years to come, it is the best predictor we have.

Of course all these Internet calculators provide just ballpark numbers — something to show you if you are even close to being on track to retire when you want. For the real numbers you need real calculations done by an expert, and we'll discuss that shortly (I know, I keep promising).

Budgeting Your Savings and Your Expenses

Cessation of Work Is Not Accompanied by Cessation of Expenses
Cato the Elder

I know some people find budgeting difficult, especially some younger people who seem to rack up debt like there is no tomorrow. If you're serious about getting out of debt (or not getting into it in the first place), you may wish to investigate software programs like Quicken[10] or iBank[11] that help you track your money. You can also take a look at the help provided by Gail Vaz-Oxlade,[12] speak to someone at your bank or talk with your accountant or financial advisor (more on this soon. Really!). But please remember that you also need to live today. Socking away every extra dollar you have into your savings will only make you resent the money you are saving at the cost of enjoying life today. So set realistic goals, both for saving and for living today.

How can you maximize your retirement with what you have already saved? Here are a few examples of what my wife and I did.

Eliminate and reduce fixed expenses wherever possible.

1. I stopped watching TV years ago, and while my wife enjoyed one or two shows a week, she ultimately realized that she could watch them on the Internet for free and so we canceled the cable. Big savings there.

2. Do you really need to get the business newspaper now that you are retired? Or could you just get it once or twice a week instead of every day?

[10] Quicken - quicken.intuit.ca/personal-finance-software/index.jsp
[11] iBank - www.iggsoftware.com/ibank
[12] Gail Vaz-Oxlade - www.gailvazoxlade.com/index.html

3. Now that you can spend more time in the garden, can you do the work your garden contractors did?

Switch to cheaper options.

1. When I retired I had to return my company cell phone. I bought a new one and consolidated it with my wife's plan and got a better combined plan than two separate plans.

2. Rather than buying private insurance from my former company's insurer, we shopped around and saved hundreds of dollars. After a year our premiums increased, so we shopped around again and got an even better deal.

3. My Mazda Miata uses premium gas and doesn't get the mileage my wife's Honda does. So for longer trips, and when it's raining and we can't put the top down, we take her car. Notice I didn't say I won't put the top down in the winter.

Me enjoying a beautiful winter's drive

4. We have a time-of-use electricity payment, so while it would be very convenient to wash clothes during the day when we are home, we wait until after 7:00 p.m.

5. We search the food ads more now that we have the time to go to multiple stores and plan our meals around the specials. And we purchase only in-season food. Sure, it would be nice to eat strawberries in December, but aside from the higher price for out-of-season food, you know the flavour just won't be there. Another example: I don't care to pay $3 for a head of lettuce in February, so when we are out for dinner, I'll order a salad, something I rarely order in restaurants.

Maximize the value.

1. There is so much we can do with our time that we can be choosy. Live amateur theatre in modestly-priced, intimate venues can be just as rewarding (and in many cases more rewarding) than the pricey big productions.

2. Eating in moderately-priced restaurants can be more fun and more satisfying than spending twice or three times that for a marginally better meal in a "premium restaurant."

3. Once we felt comfortable with what we learned from our personal fitness trainer, we diverted the money we paid her to other activities, like dance and Spanish lessons.

Reduce, Reuse, Recycle, and my personal favourite: Refuse.

1. Buy less stuff. How much more do you really need? I've been refusing to buy stuff for years, especially stuff that runs

counter to my values. For example, I refuse to buy over-packaged stuff, especially the packaging that requires any kind of tool just to open it, like the hard plastic packages that needs scissors or a knife.

2. Recycle. When my father-in-law retired, they still wanted to buy us birthday and Christmas presents. A couple of years after his retirement, I convinced them that if they really wanted to give me a gift that I would cherish, give me something that they had in their home that they enjoyed. At first they asked me to tell them what I wanted from their home, but I stood firm and told them that they had to choose, and they got the message. Not only did they not spend more money, but those things that brought them joy now bring us joy. And while they were still alive, they saw those things every time they came to visit us. What things do you have in your home that your children, or perhaps grandchildren, would love to have in their home?

Saving To Spend

Remember Aesop's tale of the ant and the grasshopper? The ant saved food for the winter, but the grasshopper didn't? Hopefully you've been saving like the ant. You've watched your nest egg grow until you are financially fit to retire. The next step is going to be tough, really, really tough. Like the ant, when winter arrives, you have to eat what you've stored away. And like the ant, you have to watch your nest egg shrink. At this point, it is going to be very easy to panic and start thinking of going back to work to keep that nest egg growing. Or you might hit the kids up for a loan that you'll repay when the market comes back (ya, sure you will). You might even sell the St. Bernard now that he's eating you out of house and home.

But if you've done your homework and kept to your plan, you'll be okay, because if you prepared well, the plan is for your nest egg *to shrink*. You have to keep that in mind every time you spend money. Are you thinking about postponing that trip to Mexico or that cruise around the Med because right now, you'd rather save that money? Well if your plans included these trips as part of your retirement, you have already saved the money, and it is now time to spend it. Also consider that if everything else is as it should be (your investments are doing okay, inflation is where you guessed it would be), then now's the time to take those trips, to buy that car, or to find the St. Bernard puppy you always wanted and have planned for. Denying yourself now may extend your money by months or years, but is that what you'll want when you're 95? I ask you: Did you save enough money for a trip to Mexico? You planned for the trip now, so make that trip now.

Speaking of taking those trips now, don't forget that travel health insurance premiums will do nothing but increase as you age. I truly hope you are able to travel in your 80's and your 90's, but the health insurance premiums might be the largest cost of the trip.

And not to belabour the point, but if you have a partner today, take that trip today. There will come a time when you may be single, and aside from the possible lack of desire to travel by yourself, the "single supplement" is an expense that you may not wish to pay.

Hey Big Spender. Spend Now, Spend Later - Big Ticket Items

Something to consider is buying big ticket items before you retire. When you are working and money is still coming in, buying a new bed or renovating the kitchen can be a bit easier because you don't have to touch your savings.

Figure out how long you need to work to pay for each item and when you think you'll actually need to make the expenditure. Let's assume you net $500 per week after all your regular living expenses, and you have the following expenses you know you'll need to make either before your retirement or shortly after:

Item	Last Repaired/ Replaced	Repair/Replace /Purchase	Estimated Cost	Work Equivalent (at $500/ Week)
Roof	2001	2016	$8,000	16
Furnace	1997	2017	$7,000	14
Bed	2000	2016	$1,000	2
Dishwasher	2003	2018	$700	1.5
Anniversary Trip to Mexico		2017	$10,000	20
St. Bernard Puppy		Right now!	$1,500	3
Totals			**$28,200**	**58.4 Weeks**

Table 1: Expenses Planning

From Table 1, we see that if you want to start your retirement with all these things looked after, and you don't want to take any money from your savings, you'll need to work another 58 weeks. Obviously there is a spectrum here: At one end, you retire today and the $28,200 comes from your savings. At the other end, you work another 58 weeks and don't touch your savings until you retire with all these things paid for. And then there is any point in between, for example, you could work another 3 weeks, buy the St. Bernard and retire. Is this a reasonable thing to do? Only you (and your partner) can answer this question. My wife and I compiled this type of table before we retired, and as it turned out, I extended my working life by about one year. Not too bad considering that we only started planning for all these things the year before I retired (when I was 59). Had we planned for it when I was 55, I may have been able to retire a bit earlier. I've included a blank worksheet for you at the end of this chapter.

Insurance

Something my wife and I really didn't plan for until almost the last minute was insurance. The company I worked for had a fantastic insurance plan, and we didn't really realize it until we had to pay for the insurance ourselves. I'm talking about dental, eyeglasses, prescriptions, travel, and the extras that the provincial health plan doesn't cover.

As a Canadian (and I'm sure many other non-Americans find this too) I'm completely baffled by the US system. The best advice I can offer is for you to seek out a local expert to help you.

Some company insurance plans allow you, as a soon-to-be-former employee, to remain with the insurance company without a health check. You take out a new policy with the same insurance company, but you don't need a physical. The premiums are based on a health questionnaire. This can be very important if you are not in the best of health because you would typically pay a premium for pre-existing conditions. Check with your employer before you retire because there is usually a time limit on this. There can be a downside to this: Compared with other insurance companies, your former company's insurance may have higher premiums, may only have a single plan that you can buy and that plan may be too much or too little for your needs. Shop around and find out what will be right for you, and don't leave this too late. My wife and I really didn't do enough to assess what we really needed, and did it too late. So we selected a plan that was a bit more costly than we needed and it didn't really match what we needed.

When you turn 65 in Ontario, the provincial health plan starts paying for some prescription drugs. The provincial government of the day has been known to change the rules, so find out if your current drugs are covered and by how much. Learn about deductibles and find out what your pharmacy's dispensing fee is. It's highly competitive out there, so educate yourself.

We will discuss your health in the next chapter, but for the moment, let's consider your current health as it applies to insurance. If you are lucky enough to have won the health lottery and you do all the right things (don't smoke, drink moderately, exercise regularly, eat well, don't take any medications), then you might want to consider insuring yourself. You can set up a separate nest egg for those items that are not covered by your provincial insurance. After all, buying insurance is a gamble, and if you are generally healthy, you might want to consider this. I travelled around the world for my employer for 13 years. They insured me for just about every travel and health contingency, and yet, in 13 years I only got sick once (from a pizza in San Jose, Costa Rica — yes, I know. Who goes to Costa Rica to eat pizza?) and I was still able to train my customers the next day between sipping sweetened tea and running to the bathroom. I only once had a medical emergency, which was on my penultimate training gig in Seattle, Washington. My ears refused to pop when we landed, and the pressure just kept building. I phoned my doctor, and he said there was nothing he or any one else could do and that it would just go away by itself. And it did, 4 weeks later. The point is that after almost 1,000 trips to over 25 countries in 13 years, the insurance company made out very well with me in not having to pay a single claim. So it boils down to "how healthy are you?" and "are you willing to take the chance?"

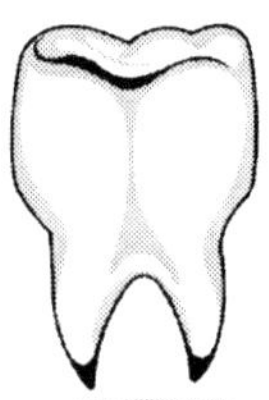

Are your teeth in great shape? Then you won't need to spend the $1,500 for a root canal or the $1,200 for a crown for each tooth. Do you have reasonably good blood pressure? Then you won't need to spend $1.00 a day for prescription drugs to keep it under control.

The only insurance you will need is travel insurance, and with your great health, it will be quite inexpensive. So if you are healthy and a chance-taker, then you might choose to "pay as you go" and basically insure yourself. Remember that medical expenses can be claimed on your income tax.

My wife and I contacted a number of insurance companies and selected the policy that seemed to make the most sense for us. Our teeth are pretty good. Our eyes are pretty good. Our overall health is pretty good and we are both physically quite fit. We have a few complaints that I'll address in the chapter on physical fitness, but nothing major. We got a plan that covers most of the basics, and it also covers us for most of our travel insurance needs. It also provides good coverage should an unexpected issue create larger health care needs. We can also purchase additional coverage for those extended trips. Notice that travel insurance premiums will just keep going up as you age, so it is another incentive to do most of your international travel early in your retirement years. It will be a few years yet before the cost of international travel insurance has us choosing Penticton, British Columbia as our winter getaway, but it is definitely in the cards.

By the way Penticton is a great town and so is the entire Okanagan valley - check it out if you haven't already.

There is a great web site called Canadian Travel Insurance Review[13] that compares most (if not all) insurance companies for you. You must check it out.

[13] Canadian Travel Insurance Review - www.travelinsurancereview.ca/

Shop around and ask questions, not only about premiums but also about coverage. And for heaven's sake, read the fine print. Not only read it, understand it. And be perfectly clear on your application form, as one incorrect or incomplete answer could cost you big time should your insurance company deny a claim because in their opinion you answered a question wrong. The media is full of horror stories about people out of their province or out of Canada who needed medical help and got home to find that their provincial insurance (or even their top-up insurance) wouldn't cover them, and they are out tens if not hundreds of thousands of dollars.

For the rest of us who didn't win the health lottery and face risks regardless of our healthy choices, insurance can be pretty expensive. Do the research now, before you retire, and keep watching the specials once you've bought the insurance. Most insurance companies offer loyalty discounts; the longer you are with them the larger the discount. But sometimes it really does pay to change companies.

Professional Help - As I Promised

I am an advocate of the notion that we all excel at something, and that we all can't excel at everything. I also believe that I get paid for doing what I excel in, and so I will pay others for doing the job in which they excel.

In this chapter, I'm going to concentrate on just one group of professionals, financial advisors (I include accountants in this group). I'll speak about lawyers in the Emotionally fit chapter, and it will become clear later why I did.

I don't have the expertise, aptitude, time or interest to do everything my financial advisors do for me. Not only do they manage my existing investments, but they also find new investments and suggest dropping investments that are not performing as well as they once did. Most importantly, they understand who I am, what my goals are, what my risk tolerance is and any number of other things about me that they use to advise me. They know us well enough that when a friend tells us about an investment his advisors suggest he buy, our advisors might feel that it isn't a good fit for my wife and me, and advise us against it. Best of all, they are not emotionally involved with my investments the way I am and can look at my investments from a detached point of view.

As we approached retirement, our financial advisors had us fill out a questionnaire that covered things like our values, our hopes and our dreams. Based on our answers, they created a plan, or roadmap, for our financial future as well as a very accurate profile. The really nice part of this is that the questionnaire was thorough enough that we felt very comfortable that the results were an accurate reflection of who we are, and so are comfortable with the plan they worked up for us. And of course, there's a lot of flexibility in the plan should our circumstances change. By the way, having a plan is also incredibly important for your emotional fitness, which we discuss later. That is, it is a lot easier sleeping at night if you are confident that you have a plan and it meets your needs.

I strongly encourage you to get a financial advisor. Let me draw a distinction between financial advisors and investment brokers, as I understand it. Investment brokers will help you choose where to put your money and even take into consideration things like your risk profile, goals and values. But financial advisors will go far beyond this by educating you and spending time with you in regular reviews and planning sessions. They will advise you which assets to sell, in what order, during your retirement to minimize taxes and maximize cash flow. They will chart out your path based on your stated spending goals, and they will be a calming voice when everyone around you is in panic mode (remember the world in 2008? and Greece in 2015?).

Don't get me wrong, investment brokers provide a very valuable service; however, they make the assumption that you are knowledgable enough to manage your own assets and don't need the handholding that a financial advisor can give you.

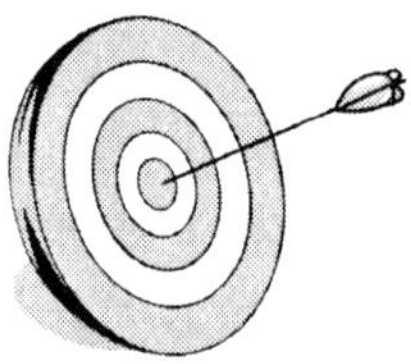

But don't just pick an advisor from the phone book (Ha! When was the last time you used a phone book? Some readers may not even know what a phone book is) or searching on the Web. Ask your friends, family, co-workers, etc. who they use. Then interview them: What is their investing philosophy, what standard services do they provide, what extras can they provide? How do they tailor their advice to you? And do you like them as people? Do you respect them? Do you think you will listen to their advice next week and for the next 20 years? Yes, 20 years, you want this to be a long-term relationship. After all, you are entrusting your money and your future to them. Don't rush into this, but do it sooner rather than later. I have the greatest respect for the abilities of my financial advisor team. They have looked after our investments for more than 20 years now. They know us and have the ability to act as our sober second thought (no, not senators, please). That is, if we were to phone them up one day and tell them we need a bucket of cash to buy a sailboat, they would probably ask us a lot of questions designed to make us think twice (and three times) before they actually sold off our investments. And they would do that because they know who we are and what our plans are; that is, we don't sail, and we don't make huge purchases like this. Sure, they'd cut us a cheque for any amount we have invested with them, but they watch out for us and would question any unusual requests we might make. And this would be a very unusual request indeed.

The First Date

Even with a good reference, you still want to form your own opinion of a prospective financial advisor. Here is a list of questions to ask a potential financial advisor on the first date (you'll find this list in the worksheet section at the end of this chapter):

- How will you determine my goals and aspirations?
- How will you determine my tolerance for risk?
- How many clients do you have?
- What is their average net worth?
- What percentage of your clients have as much money as I do?
- What services do you provide or can you arrange (accounting, legal, etc.)?
- How are you compensated? How much and when do I pay for your services?
- Will I deal with you or will I deal with your underling(s)?
- How often do we meet?
- What is your investing strategy? Or do you tailor it to each client?

- How old are you, and when will you retire? (It's always nice to have someone younger than you so they won't retire until well after you do.)

I'm sure you'll think of one or two more questions to add to this list.

Speaking of engaging professional people who are younger than you are, you might want to consider this strategy when you choose your next doctor, dentist, barber/hair stylist, etc. It is nice to know that these people will be here a lot longer than you will be and so when they retire, you'll be long gone.

After your interview you'll want to sit down and really think about the people you just met and review the answers to your questions above. You'll also want to ask yourself the following questions:

- Do I like this person?
- Will I take advice from this person?
- Do I respect this person and trust him / her with my life savings?

Finally, you'll want to take into account the recommendations you've received from others about this person.

Once you've settled on your financial advisors and asked them to make a plan for you, make a list of questions to ask them, above and beyond the really obvious one of "when can I retire?" Here is a list of questions you may already know the answers to but may want to double-check with your advisor:

When questions:

- When can I retire?

- When will the government funding start?
- When will the government funding end?
- When must we convert our RRSPs (Registered Retirement Savings Plans) into RRIFs (Registered Retirement Income Funds)?
- When do I stop paying into CPP (Canada Pension Plan)?
- When should I start collecting CPP and OAS (Old Age Security)?
- When does the government begin paying for prescriptions? How much do they pay?
- When does the government begin paying for glasses / dental? How much do they pay?

What questions:

- What government funding will we get?
- What limitations are associated with the government funding?
- What about E.I. (Employment Insurance)? Can I collect it when I retire? For how long?
- What if I work part time — what happens to medical, CPP, OAS?

How questions:

- How will we pay ourselves from our savings to minimize taxes?
- How much must we convert from RRSP to RRIF?
- How do we balance our savings between RRSPs and non-RRSPs today to prepare for retirement?
- How do we balance portfolios in and out of RRSPs to prepare for retirement?
- How are minimums and maximums on RRIFS calculated?
- How do I balance withdrawals from RRSPs and non-RRSPs to minimize taxes?
- How do I set up a fund with the Charitable Gift Funds Canada Foundation, or similar?

Yes, there certainly is a lot you need to know.

Plan v.t. To bother about the best method of accomplishing an accidental result.
Ambrose Bierce - The Devil's Dictionary

What Did I just Say?

When will you die? You need to have a target life span before you can do any kind of reasonable planning. Use a couple of the many on-line calculators listed in the references section of this chapter to create a well-reasoned assumption.

Once you calculate how long you'll live and how much you want to leave behind, you need to determine how much you have, how much you'll get from your pension and how much you'll need to live on for the remainder of your life. Check out more online calculators in the references section of this chapter.

Are you going to leave anything to anyone? As you can't take it with you, you can either plan on spending your last dollar the day you die or plan on leaving something to someone. Now that you have an estimate of when you will die, you can add your savings goals into your plan on how much you want to leave, and who will get it.

Now you need to start your planning. You have some money now, you know how much you'll need to retire, and if you don't have enough then you need to make up the difference. Planning (a.k.a. budgeting) is critical so you know when you can retire.

Unless your company allows you to remain on their health and travel insurance, you will need to purchase your own. Take your time and choose wisely. And don't forget, you **MUST** read **and understand** the fine print.

Hire the professionals; a financial advisor is a must. Even if you plan on learning all you can and doing everything for yourself, these people do this for a living, and they've seen things you'll never learn by reading books or the Internet.

Financial fitness is perhaps the most important of the three fitnesses to achieve in order to actually retire, as without the money to retire, you can be the fittest person, physically and emotionally, but still need to work to pay the rent and put food on the table. So I'll encourage you to start right away. Use the calculators as I suggested, find a financial advisor, and get a good idea of where you are and where you want to be. The sooner you get this going, the sooner you can start making any changes needed to get you financially fit for your retirement.

I'm reminded that expert advice costs money on top of the money we're trying to save for retirement. It isn't easy; but consider that $2.75 (the cost of a Starbucks Tall Cafe Latte) a day is $1,000 a year. Then again, there is the old adage that you pay yourself first. From each paycheque you deduct 5% or 10% and put that towards your retirement. After the first few paycheques, you'll probably not even notice, but your savings will.

References and Worksheets

Disclaimer: I am listing the following URLs because these are the first ones I found on the Internet. I know you'll find lots more. I am not recommending them, I am only pointing out that there are a great many of these available. I take no responsibility for your success (or lack thereof) with any of the following.

By the way, all of the following URLs were working when we went to print. As we all know, web pages are always being updated and changed, so some of these links may not be active by the time you read this book. I will try to keep this list updated on my website www.howardpell.ca.

Financial Advisors

Again, my advice to you is to get recommendations from family and friends; however, here are some links for you.

CIBC Wood Gundy
https://www.woodgundy.cibc.com/wg/index.html

Canaccord
http://www.canaccordgenuity.com/

Here is a very interesting document from 2015 February that ranks the top 50 wealth professionals in Canada.
http://www.wealthprofessional.ca/news/wealth-professional-canadas-top-50-financial-advisors-188218.aspx

Life Expectancy Calculators

This is just a sampling — there are many more out there. Try different ones and take an average.

Sun Life Financial
http://www.sunlife.ca/Canada/sunlifeCA/My+financial+plan/Tools+and+calculators/Life+expectancy?vgnLocale=en_CA

Canadian Business
http://www.canadianbusiness.com/cbn-tools-life-expectancy-calculator/

Canada.com
http://bodyandhealth.canada.com/health_tools.asp?t=10&text_id=2974&channel_id=10

CCH
http://www.cchwebsites.com/content/calculators/CALifeTime.html

Project Big Life
https://www.projectbiglife.ca/life/

These calculators all come with their own disclaimer, and none of them are a substitute for an in-depth analysis by a reputable financial advisor. However, they will give you a ballpark figure that will give you an idea of where you stand.

Government of Canada
http://www.servicecanada.gc.ca/eng/services/pensions/cric.shtml?utm_source=campaign+URL&utm_medium=twitter&utm_content=000

024+20112013,+Eng&utm_campaign=Canadian+Retirement+Income+c
alculator

TD
http://retirement-calculator.tdcanadatrust.com/

Canada Life
http://www.canadalife.com/web5/groups/common/@public/doc
uments/web_content/s5_009217.htm?menuID=255

Standard Life
https://viproom.standardlife.ca/irp/home.slac?language=1&inMe
mbrNum=

BMO
http://www.bmo.com/financial-calculators/retirement-savings/

CIBC
https://www.cibc.com/ca/retirement/article-tools/rrsp-calc-intro.html

Pre-Retirement Expenses

The following table is for you to photocopy and fill out with big-ticket items you wish to purchase while you are still working. See how long you want to keep working to pay for them so you won't have to use your savings. Of course, you don't have to buy all of them before you retire — you don't even have to earn all this money before you retire. This table is only a tool to help you in your planning.

Item	Last Repaired / Replaced	Repair/ Replace /Purchase	Estimated Cost	Work Equivalent (at $x / Week)
St. Bernard Puppy		Right now!	$1,500	3
Totals				

Budget Spreadsheets

There are so many budget spreadsheets available, I don't know where to start. Perhaps the best thing for you to do is to type "budget spreadsheet" into your favourite Web search engine and find one that meets your needs. I will recommend just one for you, by Gail Vaz-Oxlade: http://www.gailvazoxlade.com/resources/interactive_budget_worksheet.html

Questions for Your Financial Advisor(s)

Photocopy these pages and take them with you on your first date with each financial advisor. Some of these questions may not apply to you, and you may think of other questions to ask. Also, your financial advisor(s) will give you answers to questions not on this list. You might want to include them here.

Financial Advisor's

Name:	Company:
Email:	Phone:

First Date Questions:

How will you determine my goals and aspirations?
How will you determine my tolerance for risk?
How many clients do you have?
What is their average net worth?
What percentage of your clients have as much money as I do?
What services do you provide or can you arrange (accounting, legal, etc.)?
How are you compensated? How much and when do I pay for your services?
Will I deal with you or will I deal with your underling(s)?
How often do we meet?
What is your investing strategy? Or do you tailor it to each client?
How old are you, and when will you retire? (It's always nice to have someone younger than you so they won't retire until well after you do.)

Financial Advisor's

Name:	Company:
Email:	Phone:

When Questions:

When can I retire?
When will the government funding start?
When will the government funding end?
When must we convert our RRSPs into RRIFs?
When do I stop paying into CPP?
When do I start collecting CPP and OAS?
When does the government begin paying for prescriptions? How much do they pay?
When does the government begin paying for glasses/dental? How much do they pay?

Financial Advisor's

Name:	Company:
Email:	Phone:

What Questions:

What government funding will we get?
What limitations are associated with the government funding?
What about E.I. — can I collect it when I retire? For how long?
What if I work part time — what happens to medical, CPP, OAS?

Financial Advisor's

Name:	Company:
Email:	Phone:

How Questions:

How will we pay ourselves from our savings to minimize taxes?
How much must we convert from RRSP to RRIF?
How do we balance our savings between RRSPs and non-RRSPs today to prepare for retirement?
How do we balance portfolios in and out of RRSPs to prepare for retirement?
How are minimums and maximums on RRIFS calculated?
How do I balance withdrawals from RRSPs and non-RRSPs to minimize taxes?
How do I set up a fund with the Charitable Gift Funds Canada Foundation, or similar?

CHAPTER THREE

Physically Fit

It sucks getting older ... but it sure beats the alternative.

My father says this whenever he does something slowly that he has always done quickly, like when walking from the 17th hole to the 18th tee.

I'm getting on, you know.

My father-in-law would say this in similar circumstances.

And some days I know exactly what they both were talking about.

Introduction

How much would you pay to extend your life if your doctor diagnosed an untreatable condition? How much would you pay to be pain-free? How much would you pay to be healthy? How much would you pay in veterinarian bills to keep your St. Bernard healthy? What would you pay to be sure your body is physically able to do all the things you want to do once you have the time to do them in your retirement? I'm guessing you'd pay just about anything that was asked of you.

I know you exercise your St. Bernard every day and feed it nutritious food to keep it healthy, so why not yourself? In this chapter we look at getting and keeping as physically fit as you possibly can. After all, you're no spring chicken, and it has taken a good many years to get where you are today. As your retirement calculator shows, you've got many years ahead of you once you retire - will they be "good" ones or not? Or will you rapidly move into "geezerhood"?

We'll talk a little about nutrition and food and if there's life after Timmy's. We'll try to understand where you are today and how you'll go from your current level of physical fitness to where you'd like to be for your retirement. And we'll talk about getting professional help. Yes, you can benefit from a personal fitness coach. Lastly, I'll talk a bit about what happens if you didn't win the health lottery.

Don't forget to turn to Appendix A and photocopy the plan. Then as you read through the book you can update your plan.

YOLO - You Only Live Once

This is it.
No instant replays.
No Mulligans.
No second chance.
We are all given just one life, so make the most of it. Get healthy, stay healthy and start today.

Is getting and staying healthy easy? It is for some, or at least they make it look easy. For some of you, it is second nature to be fit, or active in sports, or wise in your food choices. For most of us, getting fit isn't as easy. When it is -20°C outside and I'm warm and cozy in bed, it takes a huge effort to get up and drag myself, and my wife, out of bed and to the gym at 6:30 a.m. But once I'm there, WOW, I feel great. (Okay, I'll admit it: Some days it is my wife that does the dragging.)

By getting physically fit, you'll feel better, which in turn will make you look better, which in turn will make you feel better; a virtuous circle. Your clothes will fit you better, you'll move better, you'll think better, and after all, isn't that how you want to spend your life, especially your remaining years?

You Are What You Eat

Is nutrition easy? It appears to be for some, but for most of us we need to work at it. Sure, it is easy to go out and get some fast food or order a pizza to be delivered, and every once in a while as a special treat, that's okay, but not every day. And yes, preparing three meals a day takes time and planning, but it is so rewarding. As you know, it takes planning and effort to get and stay healthy, but just remember that in the entire history of humankind, you are part of one of the first generations to have the luxury, and the choice, of living a healthy life. For almost all of our ancestors, going far back into history, their manual labour ruined their bodies. And for the women, having a dozen children on top of manual labour virtually guaranteed a short life. For the most part, their food was bland and monotonous and took hours to prepare: gather firewood and water; forage for vegetables or hunt or fish, bring it all back and cook it. Today, in Canada, we eat foods our ancestors couldn't have dreamt of, and most of it is prepared for us. No hunting and gathering for us — just open a box and toss it in the microwave; easy, but not necessarily healthy. Or better yet, just sit down and tell the waiter what you want. Again, eating in a restaurant every now and then is just fine, but not every day; Why? All that extra sugar, fat and salt that makes those restaurant meals so tasty will surely creep up and not only hit you, but stay with you.

So what's the alternative? Cooking for yourself and your family. I'm not talking about opening a few cans or boxes and adding water, or throwing something frozen into a microwave. I'm suggesting that you actually start with some raw ingredients. When we emptied out and renovated our kitchen a few years ago, the fridge and stove were moved into the dining room, while the microwave ended up in the basement. When the work crew left and we put the kitchen back together, we never brought the microwave back into the kitchen. We never use it and we don't miss it. Okay, we do use it occasionally to heat up bean-bags for sore muscles, but that's about it. Yes, preparing food is time-consuming, and you're tired after work (but you soon won't be — working that is), so have some fun cooking and get healthy at the same time.

What if you don't know how to cook? Many grocery stores offer free cooking classes that you can take. There are hundreds of books on how to prepare quick, healthy, and nutritious meals. The Internet is awash in recipes, and I can only encourage you to read just one of these cookbooks and recipe websites and attempt to get into the habit of preparing nutritious meals at home. Start slowly and work into it. And try to remember that soon you'll be retired and have all sorts of time to experiment in the kitchen. Of course, not all cookbooks will teach you how to prepare healthy meals. Comfort food, while being healthy for your soul, may not be quite as healthy for your body. I'm sure you know exactly what I mean, but let me give you just one example. There is a certain restaurant in Washington D.C. that makes the best fried chicken in the universe (I'm salivating now), but your cardiologist (yeah, yours) asked me not to disclose the name to keep you from the temptation. If I eat fried chicken once a year, that's fine; once a week isn't.

> I told you earlier that I liked fly fishing and fly tying. Something you may not know is that there are more fly tying cookbooks (books that teach you how to tie flies) than there are food cookbooks! And you know how many food cookbooks there are.

As we know, preparing good food does take a little bit of planning. If you'd like beans for tomorrow, you probably want to soak them over-night. Yes, opening a can is easier, but you also get all the added stuff you may not want, like preservatives and salt. Dry beans are cheaper too. Trent Hamm did the research for us and gives it to us on his web site.[14] The dollar savings aren't huge, but they add up, and you get the benefit of eating just the beans. I love baked beans. I soak them over night, put them in a pot in the morning with a few other ingredients, and we are eating them for lunch, with the added bonus of smelling them cook all morning.

Howard's Baked Beans

1/2 cup white beans
1/4 cup red kidney beans
1/4 cup black beans
200 g double-smoked bacon or ham
1 whole onion, peeled
1 tablespoon brown sugar
1 tablespoon maple syrup
1 tablespoon prepared mustard
2 cloves
2 bay leaves
2 tablespoons tomato paste
1/2 teaspoon very hot chili power

Soak beans over-night.
Pre-heat oven to 150 °C / 300 °F.
Drain beans and put into bean pot with everything else and mix well. Boil enough water to just cover and pour over contents. Bake until done (about 5 hours). Check every hour or so and top up with water as needed. Check seasoning before serving.
Enjoy!

[14] http://www.thesimpledollar.com/dry-beans-or-canned-beans-a-cost-effective-comparison/

How much time did it take me? About 1 minute to start them soaking before bed and about 10 minutes to put them, and other ingredients, into a pot in the morning. Really, not that much longer than opening and heating a can of beans. Yes, I had to plan it, but look at the results: A) cheaper, B) you know exactly what is in there, C) you get to smell them all morning, and D) you have a real sense of accomplishment.

Here is another great web site, $5Dinners,[15] that offers some terrific ideas on low-cost meals you prepare yourself. They also offer tips on how to shop for fresh foods and who has what on sale (although it is for American and not Canadian stores).

Two more resources that will guide you include Eat Right Ontario[16] and Canada's Food Guide.[17] Reviewing them is well worth the time.

Are you tired of preparing the same old meals? Want to spice it up a bit? Try some of the many "ethnic" cooking sites on the Internet. Do you love Indian food? Then Titli's Busy Kitchen[18] is for you. There are tons more.

Lose Weight With This Amazing Calorie Reduction Secret

Please don't tell anyone this amazing secret to reducing your caloric intake, but I'm going to show you how you can cut out 1,378 calories a day right now.

[15] www.5dollardinners.com/
[16] http://www.eatrightontario.ca/en/default.aspx
[17] www.hc-sc.gc.ca/fn-an/food-guide-aliment/index-eng.php
[18] http://titlisbusykitchen.com/

Did you know that the Tim Horton's Bagel B.E.L.T.® you ate for breakfast had 540 calories! And the mid-morning snack of a honey cruller donut sports 310 calories? Add in your two large double-doubles and you've just consumed:
Bagel = 540 calories
Donut = 310 calories
Breakfast Coffee = 264 calories
Snack Coffee =264 calories
Grand total = 1,378 calories in just ONE day!

Are you kidding me? 1,378 calories just like that? Would I kid you? Check it out at Tim's web site.[19] Did you know that Health Canada recommends[20] that for a 51-70 year old male with an active lifestyle (that's me) I should be eating 2,650 calories per day? Seems a tad high to me, but if they say so ... My fitness coach suggested that I should be around 2,000 calories per day, but for the sake of argument let's go with Health Canada.

If I had eaten the bagel and donut and drank the 2 coffees mentioned above, that would be just over half my daily allowance, leaving me just 1,272 calories for my lunch, supper, and midnight snack. That's it!

And if you are a woman my age but leading a sedentary life, your daily allowance is only 1,650 calories, and so you now have just 272 calories left over for the rest of the day. That's just one more double-double.

So if you cut out your daily Tim's run and opt to drink the coffee at the office or at home, you also cut out the temptation to eat sugar and fat. And with coffee you make at home you can learn to drink it

[19] www.timhortons.com/ca/en/menu/nutrition-and-wellness-search.php
[20] www.hc-sc.gc.ca/fn-an/food-guide-aliment/basics-base/1_1_1-eng.php

Daily Calories - Male 51-70 Years Old

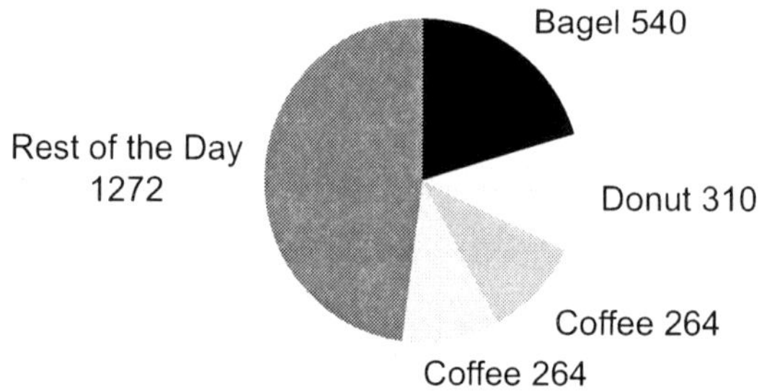

black for a whopping 0 calories per cup! I learned to drink black coffee and black tea decades ago, and I love the flavour of good tea and coffee.

But wait! You say you can't live without your Timmy's? Then take a look at *Mindless Eating*[21] by Brian Lansink. He shows you how to cut up to 200 calories a day without your body noticing. He also shows

Daily Calories - Female 51-70 Years Old

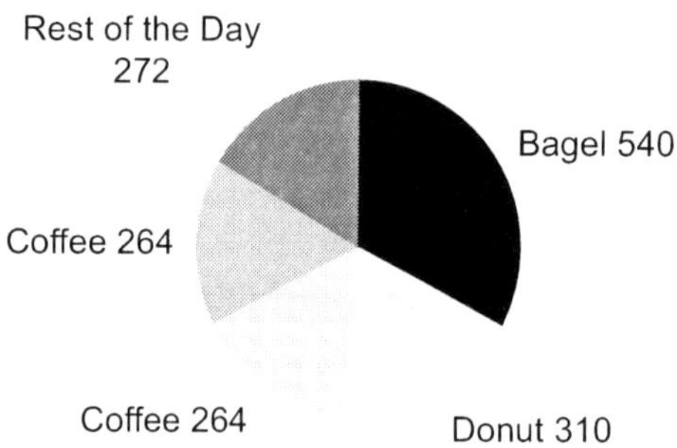

[21] Mindless Eating - mindlesseating.org/

how we get duped into eating more, and more often, as well as giving strategies on how you can recognize what's happening and do something about it.

Speaking of recipe sites on the Internet, have you seen the Paprika app? Check it out here.[22] This is one of my favourite iPad apps, and it works on just about all other platforms too. Not only does it keep all your recipes in one place, it makes shopping lists for you, allows you to search for a recipe by ingredients (what can I make with yesterday's mashed potatoes and a can of salmon? Fish cakes! Mmm) and lets you search all the recipe web sites and download the recipes right into the app for the next time you want to cook that food. I use this app all the time.

> Get the grandkids involved in preparing food if they are old enough. Can they master a knife, a stove, hot liquids? Are they old enough to understand nutrition and what the information on food labels means? Not only can cooking be a lot of fun for kids, it is a great way to spend some quality time with them.

Just think, you can cook without the sugar and salt that are so prevalent in fast foods. Your body will thank you for it by feeling better and living longer.

[22] Paprika - paprikaapp.com/

"Eat Shit - Buy My Meal Cards"

Yes, that was the actual headline of an ad in the university student newspaper where I studied (how could I forget it?). Apparently, mom and dad wanted to ensure that Jr. would eat properly in his first year away from home and bought him a semester of meal cards. Apparently, Jr. had other ideas, like turning the meal cards into ready cash so he could live off pizza and beer. I wonder whatever happened to Jr. If he's still washing down his pizza with beer, he probably weighs more than his adult St. Bernard by now.

It seems that, like Jr., my Y chromosome means that I'm predisposed to liking beer, pizza and chips. Yet somehow I have managed to acquire a taste for good foods as well. I like fruits and veggies enough that when I buy them and prepare them they end up in our tummies instead of in our composter. And I even experiment with new recipes. I love Indian food and have a wonderful friend who is an Indian chef who encourages my attempts at dhal and curries (okay, my lime pickle didn't really work, but I'll try again). So what I want to say is that we all know that junk food is not going to improve our health — just the contrary. I'm not suggesting you can never eat your favourite burger again; just consider eating better to make your retirement happier. And speaking of your favourite burger, when my mother-in-law passed away and we were clearing up her things, we found her old hand-powered meat grinder that she brought from England those many years ago, and I claimed it. It took some experimenting, but I figured out how to purchase a well-marbled chuck or blade roast, grind it up, and make fantastic hamburgers (and meatloaf), just like mom (and mom-in-law) used to make. No added sugar, no added salt, and freshly-ground from a single roast, that I personally washed, in a grinder that I personally washed. And I grind it minutes before it goes on the BBQ. Remember when we could cook medium-rare burgers and not worry about bacterial food poisoning, because we knew exactly where the hamburger came from? (No, that isn't a misprint, we all know where hamburger comes from). You really can go home again. Yum.

That's all I have to say on nutrition. You know all this already — I'm just encouraging you to put it into practice.

Are You Physically Fit For Your Retirement?

Unless you plan on parking your butt on the couch for your retirement, and the only exercise you'll do is getting up for a beer and chips, or making room in your ever-expanding body for more beer and chips, you need to be in shape to retire. What does being physically fit really mean? To some it means being a good weight for your height (Body Mass Index, or BMI) so you have a lower risk of heart disease, diabetes, bad knees, etc.

BMI is your weight in kilograms divided by the square of your height in metres. It is an *indicator* of your body fat. The ranges normally given are:
Below 18.5 - you are underweight
18.5 - 24.9 - you have a healthy weight
25.0 - 29.9 - you are overweight
30.0 and above - you are obese

There are many BMI calculators on the Internet, and some even use US measurements. Search for "BMI Calculator".

To me, *physically fit for retirement* includes having a good BMI, but more importantly, it means *being able to do the things you want to do* — play golf, bowling, tennis, or running up the steps to the Philadelphia Museum of Art that Rocky Balboa ran up. And you do it without having to stop to catch your breath. Can you walk back down these steps without your knees hurting, your hips hurting, your ankles or feet hurting? Can you walk up and down these steps without holding a handrail? Can you walk through a museum for an afternoon? A cathedral? An art gallery? A castle? Could you run at top speed for a full 5 minutes to catch your cruise ship that's leaving without you if you happen to spend a few extra minutes over your after-dinner drink?

Was that too strenuous? How about stepping into a bathtub without losing your balance? How about carrying a week's groceries, a sack of potatoes or onions from your door to your kitchen? How about pushing the lawn mower or spending an afternoon digging in the garden? What about chasing your grandchildren for a weekend while your daughter and her husband get some quiet time? Or walking your St. Bernard that is now bigger than the average European refrigerator? Do those things sound too easy for you? Were they too easy for your parents? For your grandparents? When I was in my early 20s, my grandfather was in his early 60s. He and I walked to his bank one day, and I set off at a reasonable pace for a

20-something and left him, a 60-something, in my dust (completely unintentionally as I hadn't realized what a fairly sedentary life and pack of smokes a day had done to him). Last week I played golf with my 87-year-old father, and sometimes it was me that had to keep up with him!

What do your retirement plans include? If they include aggressive sports, are you fit enough to play tennis or hockey without injury? Does walking barefoot on the sand tire you out after a few metres? Do your retirement plans include running a marathon, hiking the Chilcoot, West Coast, or Bruce trails? Are you fit enough for the kayaking, dancing, canoeing, skiing, cycling you want to do?

If you don't believe you are fit enough to do the things you want to, then now is the time to start getting physically fit for your retirement. And I really mean now! This week! Today! Finish reading this chapter, get dressed and haul your tonnage down to the closest gym.

How Long Will It Take You To Get Fit?

If you are one of those who recognize you have a way to go to be the optimum fitness for your retirement, you know that it will take some time to get where you want to go. How long depends on a few things:

- "How **big** are your **goals**?" This quote is from my fitness coach. (I love my coach for this quote. Read it again — she's so kind and sweet.)
- How much time each week are you able (or willing) to devote to getting fit?
- Will you attempt to do this on your own or will you get a fitness coach?

- Will you really become a member of the gym or will it only be your credit card that joins?
- When will you actually start to get fit? I urge you to start today.

Ultimately, the question of *how long* depends on how much you're willing and able to do. That is, can you find a 1-hour time slot three days a week to meet with your fitness coach? Can you find an additional 1-hour time slot to go to the gym two more days a week to work out without your coach? Are you able to quit smoking right away? Are you able to cut back eating fast food right away and start cooking for yourself again? Can you at least give up your daily two or three double-doubles and chocolate glazed? There was a fellow at my gym a couple of years ago who was grossly overweight (he had "big goals"). He only ate fast food, and it showed. He joined the gym and stopped eating fast food, cold turkey. Within months he had shed over 40 kilos! Not so much from exercising, which of course helped, but from eating good food. The exercising was a bonus to get his heart and lungs working optimally again. He still had a long way to go, but he was well on his way.

Obviously, the key is for you to start right away and to keep going with your fitness/health plan. You want to be physically able to enjoy all these things you have planned for, with all the money you've saved for your retirement. Get fit now.

It Isn't Going To Happen Over Night

No matter when you start, you have to realize that this is a slow process. That is, it has taken a long time for you to get where you are today, and depending on where you are today, it may take quite a while before you start seeing any improvement in your health. I led a rather sedentary life for the 20+ years leading up to my retirement. The most exercise I got was running through airports catching connections to my next training gig. So after 20 years, I had to face the fact that I couldn't expect to be healthy in weeks or even months. It would be a slow process of a couple of years. Yes, that's right, for me it was years. It may be years for you, but it may also be months if you've been more active or are in better shape than I was.

Just to give you a sense of where I started and where I am today, listen to this; on my first day at the gym, my coach tested my abilities to see where she would start me. She had me do a lunge — well, I tried to do a lunge and fell over. So she had me steady myself against the wall and do it again. How many could I do? As I recall, I managed two before I had to stop and catch my breath. Two! That's all. Today I can do walking lunges with weights, up and down the length of the gym.

Next she had me do squats. Again, I did two, steadying myself against the wall with a stability ball (again so I wouldn't fall over). It took almost two full minutes for me to catch my breath and for my heart to stop racing. Today I can do multiple squats in a squat rack with my own weight on my shoulders.

When I started, I wasn't really that overweight, but I could stand to lose a few kilos. Today I'm still a little overweight, but then again, I do like eating good food and drinking good wine. But, most importantly, today I have great balance, a strong body, pretty good lungs and a strong heart.

I don't say any of this to brag, only to encourage you and prepare you for the fact that it may take longer than you expect. If I can do it, you can do it.

Professional Help

As I mentioned before, I am an advocate of the notion that we all excel at something, and with that, we can't excel at everything. Here I'm talking about hiring a personal fitness coach. And before you skip over this section, please give me a chance to answer your objections.

> I know a few people, a very few people, who are truly motivated when it comes to their health. They educate themselves on healthy eating and healthy exercise, and then they go and do it. I wish I was one of them, but I'm not. If you are one of these people, then I take my hat off to you — you are a great role model for the rest of us. If you are not one of those people, I hope the rest of this section helps you attain the level of physical fitness you want and need for a long and healthy retirement.

Objection 1: A fitness coach is too expensive.

We are talking about your health here. Think about what you would pay to be healthy if you were lying in a hospital bed and couldn't move — probably just about anything that was asked. Your health and fitness should be the most important aspect of your retirement.

Scratch that; now that I re-read the previous sentence, I realize I should have written "your health and fitness should be the most important aspect of your **LIFE**." Without your health, your retirement will be spent cooling your heels while reading outdated magazines in various doctors' overcrowded waiting rooms with a lot of other sick people coughing and sneezing on you. Not a pretty prospect.

A personal coach will not only raise the probability that you will achieve your goals (it is still up to you to do the actual workout), but will greatly reduce the time it will take. Seriously — your coach knows how to get the most out of the equipment and how to progress you as quickly as possible based on your current fitness needs. There's more: your coach will have you doing exercises that are right for your body's limitations — that is, you'll get a plan that is personalized for you, just like your financial plan. And as an added bonus, your coach will minimize the risk of you injuring yourself. The gym is full of equipment that can seriously hurt you if you don't respect it and know how to use it. Not only will you gain confidence in using the equipment at the gym, but you will also gain confidence in your own abilities to do things that will actually give you results in return for your precious time and effort. I can't think of anything more dangerous than lying on my back on a bench with 50 kilos on a bar held over my teeth or my throat. We've all seen the YouTube videos of guys preparing to make the next payment on their dentist's BMW by failing at bench pressing in their basement; get a professional to show you the correct way to exercise.

Let me assure you that hiring a coach doesn't have to be a really long-term commitment. If you are a quick learner, make notes of what you're learning and work out on the days you don't meet with your coach, you can learn enough to fly solo fairly quickly. How quickly will of course depend on you.

So whether we are talking about time or money, the cost of a coach is worth your good health.

Objection 2: I don't want to look like those oiled-up body builders — that's gross.

Trust me, you won't. Those people spend eight hours a day, seven days a week in the gym and eat stuff you would never consider eating. Instead, you will spend one hour a day, three or four days a week with your coach, and then another hour or two, one or two days a week exercising on your own. What you will hopefully end up looking like, and this will take a lot of effort on your part, is a healthy, strong, vibrant person. Look around the gym; in my gym the people who look like me (slightly overweight but getting fit) hugely outnumber the really buff bodybuilder types (men and women). And yes, there are those really buff bodybuilder types at my gym, but I recognize that I will never, ever look like them because I neither exercise nor eat like them.

And I promise you, if you ever start looking like a body builder and you don't like it, you can always change your workouts.

Objection 3: I'll buy a treadmill for home — it's cheaper.

They have loads of treadmills at the gym, plus tons more equipment your coach will train you to use effectively. Some of the equipment is for cardio (like a treadmill), some not — and you can't just do cardio exercises to get fit, you need to strengthen all your muscles. Besides, do you know how boring a treadmill is? It is one step up from watching paint dry. Sure, you'll use it in your basement for a while, but then you'll find other uses for it, like storing the Christmas decorations for 10 months each year. There is also a well-known phenomenon where once you get to the gym, you gain motivation. You gain it from seeing all the other people exercising. The peer pressure of you being there means you can't just stand around looking at muscle mags — you get to work. You also gain motivation by moving your body. Honestly, get moving, and you feel good. Your blood moves, you breathe deeply, you feel more alive.

Still not convinced? Check out the price of a decent treadmill. The cheapest one I've seen at Canadian Tire is $1,000. Their best is just over $4,000. As I write this, you can get a membership at World Gym for $10 a month. That's 33 years of membership for the price of Canadian Tire's best treadmill. And there are lots of other gyms out there as well. In fact, the closest gym to me is GoodLife Fitness, and I really like it there. It is a bit more expensive, but it is clean and close to home, and being close is a great motivator on those snowy winter mornings. Again, once you pay the gym membership, they have lots of other equipment for you to use. Don't forget, most gyms also reward you after your workout by having a sauna. There is nothing like a sauna for relaxing those muscles you haven't used in the past 20 years and are just re-awakening.

Okay; If I haven't convinced you to not buy your own treadmill, could I interest you in a gently used one? You'll have to get it out of my basement. And oh, what the heck, I'll throw in the Christmas decorations, no extra charge.

Objection 4: I'm embarrassed to be seen — I don't look great in spandex.

Okay, I'll divulge the secret now: Nobody looks good in Spandex — it is all Photoshop. But you are right, you don't look like the people in the ads for gyms; they look great because that's what the ad makers want you to think you'll end up looking like. But go to the gym and check out the "before" and "after" photos of their customers. And here is what else a visit to the gym will show you; most people at the gym look exactly like you. Go to the gym and look around, and you may be surprised that many people there look like the "before" picture rather than the "after" picture. Remember, progress is slow. Besides, they are there for the exact same reason as you — to get fit and to stay fit. They are not there to look at you or anyone else. If you talk with them, they will encourage you and praise you for being there.

You will be in a very elite group, as only 15% of Canadians take their fitness seriously enough to get their weekly exercise, according to this Globe and Mail article.[23] And after you become a regular at your gym, don't feel shy about welcoming and encouraging new people to the gym. As for the spandex, give it a miss and start with some comfortable gym clothes. Oh yes; Gym clothes should not be too revealing, if you catch my drift; your primary reason for being at the gym is to get fit, not get a mate.

---

[23] Globe & Mail - www.theglobeandmail.com/life/health-and-fitness/statscan-report-says-many-canadians-not-as-active-as-they-think/article562605/

Objection 5: I tried lifting weights once, and they are really, really heavy!

Ha ha ha, yeah that's an old joke. But seriously, the whole point of a personal coach is that he or she is going to create a fitness program just for you. Your coach will ask you questions about your current health and your goals. Your coach will test your current level of fitness, and you will start slowly (like my 2 squats with a stability ball) and progress at a pace that your coach will set for you. If your coach does recommend lifting weights, then you'll start with small weights (think of lifting soup cans) and work your way up. Again, your coach's role is to ensure you get results while not injuring yourself. Once you know the correct form and the correct way to get the maximum out of an exercise, you might want to help others who you see are either going to injure themselves or aren't getting the full benefit from the exercise. If you feel you must offer advice, be kind and gentle with them. Better yet, the only advice you should give them is your success story with your coach.

Speaking of giving advice, check out these 10 Ways To Be A Gentleman At The Gym.[24] Women can also learn from these, but of course their rules vary slightly.

[24] http://www.artofmanliness.com/2008/06/29/10-ways-to-be-a-gentleman-at-the-gym/

What will it cost to get fit?

Gym clothes = $50
Gym shoes (good ones help prevent injury) = $150
Gym membership = about $1/day (as I write this, some gyms offer memberships of $10/month = $0.33/day!)
Personal trainer = $50/hour, depending upon their training and their skill level
Time (1 to 2 hours, 5 times a week) = 10 hours/week
Your good health = priceless

Choosing a Coach

Remember what I said about finding a financial advisor? Well, the same goes for finding a fitness coach. Ask around, get recommendations, then interview them. What is their background? Why are they a coach? Can they help you with nutrition? Can they help you with your golf swing, carrying suitcases or digging in your garden? Do they have any experience with coaching other people who suffer from the same ailments you do (e.g. arthritis, back problems, tennis elbow)? You are going to spend a lot of time and money with this person, and you want to get the best person for your special needs.

And just like financial advisors, fitness coaches come in all shapes and sizes. Some are more interested in bodybuilding, some are into contact sports, and some are golf enthusiasts. This isn't to say that a bodybuilder can't help you with your golf swing, but it is just one more thing to consider before you settle on a coach. And remember, you are not getting married to your coach; you can always find another coach if it isn't working out the way you want it. That is, don't be afraid of firing your coach and getting a new one if it isn't suiting you or if you get injured because your coach isn't paying attention or doesn't understand your limitations. Whatever you do, don't quit the gym because your coach isn't the perfect match for you; stay at the gym and get a new coach.

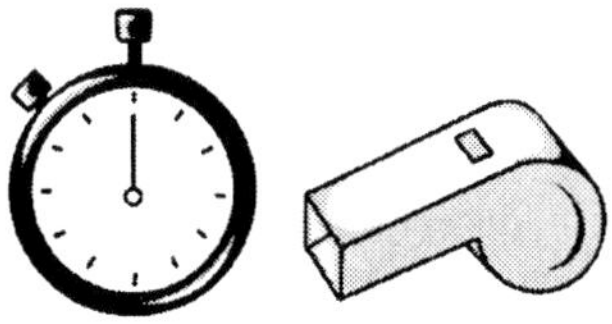

A female friend of mine has a female coach about her age, so the coach understands my friend's aches and pains and limitations. She also understands my friend's playful whining and when she isn't giving her all. And best of all, they can moan about their kids.

So far I've talked about getting physically fit from the point of view of strengthening your muscles (this includes your heart and lungs) so you can fulfil your retirement goals. I'd like to talk briefly about a slightly different kind of fitness that borders on both physical and emotional fitness. I'm talking about the fitness one gains from activities such as yoga and tai chi. This is something I have not done, but I know many people who are ardent fans. Many people have told me about the benefits they get from these activities, and this winter I plan on joining a couple of classes. It certainly sounds good to get the physical and emotional health in one package. I'll let you know.

Can I Get Fit Without a Coach?

Still sounds too expensive, or just not for you? Okay, how about this: Buy your gym clothes and good (and I mean good) shoes and check out your local walking / running clubs or biking groups, which are typically free. Look into the community centres — most offer reasonably-priced exercise classes, and some offer swimming pools. Nothing close by? Okay, grab some of your co-workers at lunch and drag them out for a walk around the office building. Challenge them to a lap around the business park, and the last one back at their desk is a Clavin (perhaps my favourite episode of Cheers!).

Watch for specials at the gym — they frequently have deals even for personal training. My sister wanted to join a gym and found a 2-for-1 deal, but she didn't have anyone to join with her. She asked the folks at the gym to let her know if anyone else showed up without a partner, and sure enough, someone did come into the gym without a partner for the 2-for-1 special. They contacted each other and set a time when they could both go in and sign up. As it turns out, they both work different shifts so never see each other, but they still got the 2-for-1 deal. And don't forget that many gyms offer free group fitness classes to members, so you will get guided instruction at no additional cost to your membership. The key point is to commit to a regular schedule and start working out with some guidance. Be sure the time you're investing really is making a positive impact and is motivating enough of you to commit time every week.

Dis-ease

So far in this chapter, I have made a huge assumption that we are all simply out of shape, some more, some less, and that all we need to do is eat healthily and exercise to regain our health. I have ignored the fact that many people "our age" may have some disease, affliction or disability that prevents them from full physical fitness. Or if it doesn't prevent them, it slows them down in attaining full physical fitness. Let me briefly address this issue here.

Let's begin with a very quick definition of "disease." A chiropractor I went to many years ago called this "dis-ease," and I really liked the term. That is, the body was not at ease for some reason, and through chiropractic care, he was going to get people back into ease. The message I want to convey is that while we all have some physical limitations the key is to do as much as you possibly can to get physically fit. This is also another plug for getting yourself a personal fitness coach, someone who has been trained in understanding the limits of certain dis-eases and then works with you to overcome those limits as best you can.

Two short personal examples, involving injury and arthritis:

It was a workout day without my coach, and she wasn't in the gym at the time. My wife and I were in the gym, and everything was going well. I was doing standing jumps onto a bench.

I had done about half the set, and for some reason my mind wandered; on the dismount, I landed with one of my feet on one of the bench's feet. Everything went into slow motion (you know the feeling) as I crumpled to the floor. My wife packed me up, and I hobbled home to ice packs, in agony, watching my ankle swell up to twice its normal size.

I phoned my trainer, and she immediately had me soaking my foot and ankle in a bucket of ice water a dozen times a day (I still get chills thinking about it). Once the swelling was down and I could walk again, she started me on the road to recovery with very specific exercises to strengthen and heal my ankle. At the same time, she made sure that I was still exercising as much of my other muscles as possible without using that ankle. That is, I was able to overcome the dis-ease.

Here's another example: I don't recall the day I woke up to discover I had arthritis in my hands, but I do remember my mother telling me that it seemed to run in the family as she showed me how it affected her. Like millions of others, I have learned to live with it and to accept that there are certain things that take me longer to do than they used to, like tying my shoelaces. But in the gym I now feel the restrictions of my dis-ease. My coach was increasing the weights for deadlifts and lat-pulldowns until one day I found that doing them just wasn't possible with the heavier weights — not because of my back, shoulder or arm muscles, but because my hands couldn't hold the weight due to the arthritis. My coach immediately saw the issue and suggested I start using weightlifting wrist straps.

She explained that everyone's hands have a limit of what they can lift, and when they reach that limit, lifting straps may be the solution. It is just that my limit is much less than someone without arthritis. So again, I was able to overcome the dis-ease. When I went into the sports store to buy the straps, I asked the two buff guys behind the counter for the straps and they chided me that I was going into the power lifting big time. I thought for a second about saying "yes I was" but reconsidered and told them about my arthritis. I think they were just a little disappointed.

I don't wish to trivialize any dis-ease you may have or say that you can overcome it with patience and practice; however, we've all seen the Internet videos of people with severe physical limitations doing remarkable things in the gym. Unless you are bedridden or permanently restricted to a wheelchair (and I've seen people do amazing workouts sitting in their wheelchairs), there is always something that you can do to improve your overall physical health. And I hope you can improve it to the point where you are fit enough to enjoy your retirement by doing those things that you want to.

To close this chapter, I'll add a word on autoimmune disorders. I'll preface my remarks by reminding you that I'm not an expert on this at all — I'm relating the following to you as I heard it from people I trust to know. These autoimmune disorders are where the body's immune system attacks and destroys healthy body tissue by mistake. There are dozens of these disorders, and they manifest themselves in different ways. In many of the ones that attack the joints and muscles, people find it beneficial to exercise gently and regularly to keep as much of their mobility as they can. That is, being sedentary to relieve the pain may not, after all, be the best thing you can do. By gentle exercising, you may be able to lessen the pain and increase mobility. For some, it hurts to work out, but if they don't, it hurts even more.

Can You Please Repeat That? Slowly.

It is cliché to say this, but you really only live once, and your health is the most important aspect of your one-and-only life. You can have all the money in the world, but without your health, you may never enjoy it. Proper nutrition and exercise is the key to your good health. I wish I could recall who said to me that they got a large income tax refund, and rather than spending it on something they really didn't need like a TV, they decided to purchase a gym membership and the service of a fitness coach. Fantastic! Unless you are incredibly motivated as well as knowledgeable about all human muscles and exercises that work those muscles, consider a fitness coach. Even if you only hire a coach for 6 months to get you on the right path, you will not regret learning everything your coach can teach you, and you'll use that guidance for years to come.

When I started with my fitness coach, I couldn't carry the laundry from the basement up two flights to the bedroom without getting winded. Today, it's a breeze. Did that happen overnight? Of course not, but it happened. Do I look like a muscle guy? My wife only wishes it were so. I'm still slightly overweight because I like to eat and drink, but I can do everything that I want to. I can walk 18 holes in the hot sun. I can work in my garden for hours on end. A couple of years ago I walked (and sweated) all over Lisbon for a week in 34°C weather with my ankles sore from arthritis, but I did it. A year

later I walked 16 km in the mountains of southern Spain; it was 400 metres up, and then 400 metres back down, all in a single day. I was exhausted by the end of the day, but I did it, and my wife was right beside me all the way. We certainly earned our vino tinto that day.

I couldn't run a marathon, but I can run for 4 or 5 minutes. I couldn't run up the Philadelphia Museum of Art stairs, but I could walk them with ease and wouldn't need to hold a handrail. Could I play hockey or football? Nope, but I would have no trouble walking a couple of blocks from my car to the top seats in SkyDome / Rogers Centre (or whatever it is called this week). I can dance all night and still ask for more.

I am fit enough to do the things I want to do. And with planning and focus, you can be as well.

References and Worksheets

Disclaimer: I am listing the following URLs because these are the first ones I found on the Internet — I know you'll find lots more. I am not recommending them, I am only pointing out that there are a great many of these available. I take no responsibility for your success (or lack of success) with any of the following.

By the way, all of the following URLs were working when we went to print. As we all know, web pages are always being updated and changed, so some of these links may not be active by the time you read this book. I will try to keep this list updated on my website www.howardpell.ca.

Links To Workout Sites You Could Do Without A Gym

Fitness Magazine - great workouts and nutritional advice.
http://www.fitnessmagazine.com/

Goodlife Fitness Facebook Page - lots of great info here
https://www.facebook.com/goodlifefitness

Fitness - Many good workouts and recipes for healthy eating
http://www.fitness.com/

Manitoba Fitness Council - Some great info on how to get started, choosing the type of fitness program that's right for you and choosing a facility. Some very good checklists on choosing these as well as choosing a fitness coach.
http://www.manitobafitnesscouncil.ca/main.asp?cat_ID=7

Meetup - Type in your city's name and what you want to do "run", "walk", "dance" and you'll be amazed at what's going on.
http://www.meetup.com/

Choosing A Personal Fitness Trainer / Coach

#1 - ask your friends and family. If you can't get a recommendation from someone you know then take a look at some of these:

GoodLife Fitness - This is the gym I go to, and I'm very satisfied with what they offer.
http://blog.goodlifefitness.com/10-10-ways-chose-personal-trainer

Ace Fitness - I don't know them, but I like what they have to say on this page
http://www.acefitness.org/acefit/healthy_living_fit_facts_content.aspx?itemid=19

Greatist - Again, I don't know them, but they do offer some advice that I agree with
http://greatist.com/fitness/how-to-choose-best-personal-trainer

Links to Recipe Sites

Before you start looking for recipes, you need a recipe app. This is my favourite, and it is worth every nickel.
http://paprikaapp.com/

I love Indian food, and Titli's Busy Kitchen has some fabulous recipes and great videos of her preparing the food (non-Indian as well). With the added bonus that Titli (not her real name) is kind of kooky. Here is the main page of her web site:
http://titlisbusykitchen.com/
And here is my favourite video of hers. No I haven't tried this recipe yet. Told you she was a bit kooky.
http://titlisbusykitchen.com/recipe/chilli-pickle

$5 Dinners - for those of us on a budget, some very low-cost meals
http://www.5dollardinners.com/

Tim Horton's nutrition information
http://www.timhortons.com/ca/en/menu/nutrition-and-wellness-search.php

CHAPTER FOUR

Emotionally Fit

Life is what happens to you while you're busy making other plans.

John Lennon

It is impossible to enjoy idling thoroughly
unless one has plenty of work to do.

Jerome K. Jerome

Introduction

Emotional fitness is how I define your mental preparation for retirement. That is, what have you done by way of planning to prepare yourself for the sudden bonus of having at least 8 hours a day, 7 days a week, every week, for the rest of your life, without the work routine and deadlines that you have lived with for your entire adult life? It will be like you are 5 years old again — you'll have nothing to do but play all day (well, not quite, but close). Suddenly, you have no responsibility to anyone but yourself (and possibly your partner). Your daily obligations, for the most part, will be self-imposed. So you must prepare for this dramatic change.

There are also other changes you will need to prepare yourself for, some subtle and, some not so subtle. If you haven't already noticed it, you will soon find new physical limitations that are going to slow you down. Yes, retirement is definitely a time of change, and good emotional fitness is important for you to be able to take these changes in your stride.

In this chapter we'll talk about preparing for the day you say good-bye to your work life and everyone and everything in it. Of course, you'll make a plan, and you'll try to stick with the plan. For some of you, there's a big change waiting for you at home, namely your partner, so you'll need to plan together for this big event. Not only will your relationship with your partner change, but your relationship will also change with other family members, your friends and your acquaintances. If you don't have a partner, then you're facing a change of not having regular, daily interactions with others. It will be just you — unless you plan for it. Your biggest challenge might just be figuring out how you are going to fill 40+ hours a week in a satisfying and fulfilling way.

Don't forget to turn to Appendix A and photocopy the plan. Then as you read through the book you can update your plan.

I Second That Emotion

As I mentioned in the introduction to this book, I like Tony Robbins' Six Human Needs:

1. **Certainty**: assurance you can avoid pain and gain pleasure
2. **Uncertainty/Variety**: the need for the unknown, change, new stimuli
3. **Significance**: feeling unique, important, special or needed
4. **Connection/Love**: a strong feeling of closeness or union with someone or something
5. **Growth**: an expansion of capacity, capability or understanding
6. **Contribution**: a sense of service and focus on helping, giving to and supporting others

The first one "Certainty" is really the only one that can be primarily addressed by financial fitness and we've covered that already. But there is an emotional aspect to certainty and that is the knowledge that everything is in place and is ready to go. So let's make sure that we are emotionally **certain** for our future and even for our survivors' futures after our death.

Emotional Health as it Relates to Physical Health

A man's gotta know his limitations.
Harry Callahan, Magnum Force

I just want to tie up a loose end I feel I left in the previous chapter on Physical Fitness. If it hasn't already happened, you will soon start to notice that you can't do some things you could before, or you can still do them but, just not as quickly or with the same dexterity. We touched on this in the previous chapter, but now I want to address the emotional side of this. That is, you are going to need to expect, and prepare for, the inevitable deterioration of your body. The aches and pains you first started to notice in your 40s and 50s were just a sign of things to come. Oh goody, goody, I can hardly wait.

For me, it is primarily my hands. The arthritis makes them stiff and slow to do the tasks I ask of them: typing, tying flies and shoelaces, gripping barbells in the gym. I'm very fortunate in that my hands rarely give me much pain, so far, and the pain is manageable. But it is my attitude towards the stiffness in my hands that is surprising me. Yes, it is frustrating when I can't open a new jar of pickles and have to resort to the jar opener gizmo my wife got at Lee Valley.[25] But what surprised me is my reaction to the experience. It punctuates the fact that I'm not young any more. That is, I don't think of myself as "old," and yet I seem to be exhibiting the signs of age, and I don't particularly like it, and I'm not completely sure I'm handling it all that well. I don't think I'm a vain man. I don't believe I've ever been called handsome or good looking, so losing my hair and gaining bags under my eyes doesn't bother me as much as gaining these new

[25] https://www.leevalley.com/

physical limitations. I can't offer you any coping strategies (see the section on Professional help at the end of this chapter) but only tell you to expect to have to deal with this. This reminds me that many years ago my wife was the Director of one of the first Independent Living Projects in Ontario, and we met many quadriplegics, some of whom became friends. One friend offered me the following advice one day: He said, "We don't consider ourselves to be disabled *per se* — we consider everyone else to be temporarily able-bodied." And he was right: If we live long enough, there will come a time when we all will have to deal with some kind of disability.

And not to belabour the point, but I'll give you a few more examples: First, my lung capacity isn't what it used to be. It might have something to do with all those cigarettes I smoked in my teens and twenties. This limits my hiking speed, the size of pack I can carry and the altitude that I hike at, but it doesn't stop me from hiking. Second, I attended too many rock concerts in the 60s and 70s, and so now I wear hearing aids. As a side benefit, it is remarkable how my hearing aids cured my wife's mumbling. A few years ago, my glasses became bifocals, and then most recently they morphed into trifocals, with separate glasses I use just for working on the computer. And then it happened: my first cataract surgery. My left eye just couldn't focus and was getting progressively worse. The surgery was easy (physically), but this was a real milestone for me, as it proved I was "getting on".

Perhaps the biggest hurdle for me was waking up one morning with an aching pain in my big toe. At first I thought I must have kicked something on my nightly sojourn to the bathroom, but it didn't get better, and a day later I saw my doctor, who pronounced the dreaded word of my entry into senior-hood: "gout".

"What do you mean, gout?" I asked. "That's what old people get, and I'm not old."

"Not at all," he explained, "People in their 20s can get it."

Somehow, that did not cheer me up. I'm happy to say that since it cleared up I've never had it again, and I hope to never have it again. It was my left foot and so made driving difficult as I couldn't use the clutch and, had I a St. Bernard, I wouldn't have been able to take it for a walk.

The point of all this is that you have to mentally prepare yourself for these physical changes. The only consolation I can give you is that you are not alone, and now I know why old people sit around discussing their operations, aches, pains and bodily functions.

So now that we've talked a little about our aches and pains, it is time to consider how we'll mentally approach our retirement and what we are going to do with our "golden years."

Ease Your Way Out

Now that you've decided it is time to stop working, think about getting ready for the reality of "being on your own." Something that may be an option for you is "easing" into retirement. I was very fortunate that my manager and the company I worked for could accommodate me switching from full-time work to part-time for the last year or so before I retired. You may not be as fortunate as I was, but it is worth considering. By reducing my work week to Tuesday, Wednesday and Thursday and having a four-day weekend, I was able to experiment with how I would fill four days a week, and I did it for over a year. Plus my wife and I learned to live on less, as my income was reduced. We earned less, spent less and saved less. It also got us out of the saving mentality, which we needed to do as preparation for the time when we would start spending our savings.

This also provided a bit of a bonus to my manager and company, as it prepared them for my inevitable departure. While I obviously can't compare easing into retirement with going cold turkey, easing out sure worked for me, and I urge you to ask your manager about it.

Exit, Stage Left
Snagglepuss

How did Snagglepuss always know when to "Exit, Stage Left"? I'm not sure, but I do know, that like Snagglepuss, you need an exit plan. And having a contingency plan is also a good idea, just in case. I started with a whiteboard in my home office and wrote down my ideal exit plan and under it, my contingency plan. I erased the board long ago, but I do recall it looked something like the following:

- Best case scenario: Change my working relationship with my company to 3 days/week for at least 1 year with reduced pay and full benefits. Use the extra time to develop my interests and prepare for my retirement.
  – If that was unacceptable to my company, then

- Change my working relationship with my company to 4 days/week for at least 1 year with reduced pay and full benefits. Use the extra time to develop my interests and prepare for my retirement.
  – If that was unacceptable, then
- Rearrange my vacation days to take 1 vacation day/week for as many vacation days I had. Use the extra time to develop my interests and prepare for my retirement.
  – If that was unacceptable, then
- Seek employment with former co-workers who had set up their own small companies and work for them for 3 days/week and no benefits.
  – If that was unacceptable, then
- Seek part time employment in another field, perhaps as a Walmart greeter or the operator of a weenie wagon.

Table 2: Sample Exit Plan

The second-to-last option would have been the hardest, not because my good friends who had started their own companies didn't need me or want me. Quite the contrary, two of them that I spoke with wanted me to start the very next day; however, they wanted upwards of 50 or 60 hours a week from me, and here I was trying to ease myself out, not in.

Did I mention that my manager and company went for my best case scenario? They were great!

I've created an exit plan guide for you in the Worksheet section of this chapter. Take your time with it, and don't forget to work in a contingency plan, just in case.

How To Live With Your Spouse Or Partner

First a word to the men reading this book, about your partner. Going back to the Temptations' *Papa Was A Rolling Stone* song, the second line in the chorus is *Wherever he laid his hat was his home*. I think that's probably true for most men; we can live just about anywhere, but with a woman it's different. There is a rocker with a worn cushion, her mother's clock that doesn't work, an old quilt that is quite worn, a few faded photos in frames, battered cookie sheets, ancient mixing bowls chipped around the edges and mismatched cups. These, and a few more known as "her own things" are needed to make a house a home for a woman. The wise man will bear this in mind as we explore this next section on how to live with your partner after retirement. Yes, I've been reminded that this is gender stereotyping and that many women are the rolling stone, but I really like the Temptations.

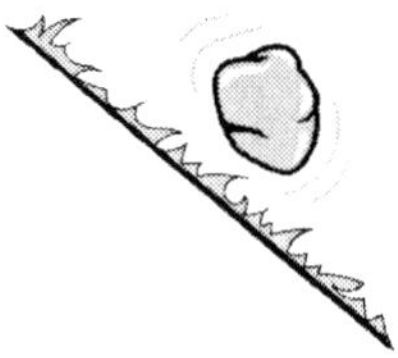

My wife and I were very fortunate — not only was I able to ease myself out of work by reducing my hours to part-time for a year, but I was also able to work from home for the last 3 years of my working life. That gave my wife (who runs her consulting business from home) and me ample time to get to know one another and learn how to live with each other 24 x 7. We weren't joined at the hip, of course, but while most people don't see their partner for 40+ hours a week, there were very few times when we were without each other's company, and that really helped us adjust. Somehow, you are going to need to adjust your lifestyle so the love of your life doesn't become the ex-love of your life.

Let's look at some different scenarios. I've listed the various possibilities in the table below.

Scenario	Your partner:	You are retired and you are:
A	Keeps Working	Busy
B	Keeps Working	Bored
C	Retires and is Busy	Busy
D	Retires and is Busy	Bored
E	Retires and is Bored	Busy
F	Retires and is Bored	Bored

Table 3: Partner Planning

The following section may be difficult for some readers. My wife and I try to share the household duties equally. It doesn't always work that way, but we try to pull our own weight where we can. I realize that some partners don't do this, and so what I have to say next may sound odd or even laughable if you happen to be the one who already does everything. Of course, those of you who are single can pretty much skip this section.

Your Partner Still Works

If your partner keeps working and you've just retired, then now is the time for you to take some of the load off your partner. It's time for you to take on more of the household chores (assuming you don't do most of them already). After all, now that you are retired, you can go shopping in the middle of the day, you have time to cook, and if your partner takes a lunch to work, you have time to prepare that lunch before they leave. You have time for laundry, cleaning, etc. Gee, isn't retirement fun? Well, cleaning isn't, but cooking can be, and running errands during the day can be, especially when you know everyone else is at work. Do you remember what it felt like when you took an "I'm sick of work day" or a "staycation" and drove around town on errands on a Tuesday afternoon, that guilty kind of feeling similar to playing hooky from school? It sure is great! Well, that feeling will wear off after a while, but I really enjoyed it when I first retired. And while I'm on the topic, vacations still feel like vacations, even though every day is a holiday (and there are many times I forget what day today is). Even taking a 2- or 3-day vacation to a beach still feels like a vacation, and we come home refreshed and raring to go again.

Scenario A)

This can be really nice for both of you. Your partner is still enjoying his/her career and you are busy. With luck, you can still meet for dinner and evenings and discuss your day. Just remember that whenever you want to schedule anything with your partner, your partner's work calendar must be considered and probably considered first. Don't get impatient — just because you were ready for retirement doesn't mean your partner is too. This can be especially true when you are ready for travel but your partner isn't or doesn't have the flexibility with their job to drop everything and take advantage of last minute offerings. By the way, this is the situation with my wife and me as I write this, and it really is working well for us. Actually she does have flexibility with her work, as she can schedule time away in exchange for reduced income; she's in the "ease into part-time" phase.

Scenario B)

This could be the worst-case scenario, where your spouse is still working (working from home will make it even worse) while you are retired and have nothing to do. I'm sure this happened all too often with our parent's generation, where the wife was a stay-at-home mom and the husband worked outside the home. When he retired with nothing to do, he trailed his wife around the house as she did her typical routine and drove her stark, raving mad by using his years of management skills to re-arrange her cupboards, her drawers and her life. Perhaps that's where the term "justifiable homicide" originated.

You've Both Retired

You have both retired and now you are ready to play. This can be a great time of your life, but only if you are both in the same frame of mind or are okay with the other person being in a different frame of mind. That is, if you are busy and your partner isn't and it irks you, you have a problem. Let's look at the scenarios.

Scenario C)

You are both retired and you are both emotionally fit and ready for a life of leisure. This is my ideal situation, and one that I hope to be in eventually. That is, my wife and I are currently in scenario A) but one day she too will fully retire and by then she will be emotionally fit for her retirement. It will give us ample time to pursue our own interests and yet still enjoy our time together.

Scenario D)

You are both retired, and your partner has all kinds of hobbies and things to do, but for some reason you find yourself at sea. Nothing interests you, nothing excites you, you don't seem to have the energy to even work on the hobbies you used to find satisfying. If your partner is okay with you mooning around the house and is patient about you finding your interests (and getting emotionally fit), then that's just dandy. But if your disinterest also leads you to drop any role in the household tasks, chances are that your busy partner is not going to be too happy. At the end of this chapter we'll talk about life coaches, and that may be an option for you.

Scenario E)

The opposite of scenario D). You are both retired and you are busy but your partner would rather sit around and read books all day (or, horrors — watch TV). If you are okay with this and are happy to go your own way, then there's no problem. Just be careful that you don't force your partner into doing something they aren't interested in doing. Try to be patient while they gain their emotional fitness. And if you must make suggestions on how they can get engaged, keep them to a minimum.

Scenario F)

You've both retired, and you're both emotionally unprepared for it. I really don't know the solution to this one other than perhaps a life coach to help you both. Of course, perhaps you are both happy to take turns holding the TV remote while the other gets another beer and feeds the St. Bernard. And if you both are happy ... good for you.

Whichever scenario you and your partner fall into, I wish you well, and I hope that you ultimately end up in Scenario C). Good luck.

Hello, Nice To Meet You, And What Do You Do?

When I was working, I had a ready answer to that question:

> "I work for the largest software company in Canada, and I develop courseware and travel the world training our customers on how to use, maintain and customize our software."

That was me for the last 20 years of my working life. And then boom! That isn't me any more. One day you will wake up and your whole identity (well, at least a very big part of your identity) is gone forever. Today, I *used* to be a software trainer. Again, I was fortunate in that I was also able to ease myself into the transition of my identity. For many, it happens all in one day.

This loss of identity is a huge stumbling block for many people when they think about their retirement. They say things like "what would I do with myself if I didn't work?" Which I believe can be translated into "*who would I be* if I didn't work?" And so they continue to work, simply because they don't want to give up their identity. Of course, some people find a huge amount of satisfaction and joy in their work and will never retire. That's great for them, but I'll bet none of them are reading this book, nor would they, even if you bought it for them and offered to look after their St. Bernard while they read it.

When you retire, your working identity is gone. Your role in the organization is no longer yours. You are no longer a welder, a mechanic, a police officer, a nurse, an admin assistant. Your authority is gone, as no one reports to you any more. Your status is gone, as you are no longer the big boss, the go-to-guy for maintenance questions or that "great gal in accounting" that everyone loved because you got their expenses reimbursed in record time. Any special privileges that came with your position are now gone: You don't fly business class any more, no more company car, no more free sports tickets, people don't buy you chocolates or a bottle at Christmas. You are now just one more of the growing number of retirees. Even if you currently have lots of external interests, when you retire your predominant daily identity is gone. You need a new identity, and it doesn't happen over night like in so many Hollywood movies where exactly 85 minutes into the movie our down-on-his-luck hero suddenly "finds" himself and his *raison d'être* and he becomes a new person. No, it takes time to create a new identity, and the time to start this transformation is now.

In the run-up years before my retirement, I became a Rotarian, not with the thought that this would be my new *persona*, but for two important (to me) reasons: 1) I wanted to give back to my local community and to make the world a better place to live and 2) after 13 years of living in hotels as I travelled the world, I found that I knew nobody in my own city and it was time for me to make some friends. However, being a Rotarian has now become a large part of my life and a large part of my identity. Around the same time I became interested in making videos, and (if I do say so myself) I've become rather good at it. I like writing the script, running the camera, directing the actors. I like the post-production aspects of editing, music, titles, etc. Again, I didn't start out in filmmaking with the idea of making it a part of my new identity — it just worked out that way.

Now when I'm asked "what do you do?" I tell people I'm a Rotarian, I'm an amateur filmmaker, and most recently, I'm a published author. I define myself by my interests and not by my job.

These are not my only interests, and some of them I do well, and others, not so well. After a career of travel, I still love to travel, but now for pleasure. I normally step on my wife's toes when we are social dancing, but I'm improving. I am also a terrible golfer but love to spend time on the course with my dad. And I rarely catch fish on the flies that I've tied, but I love standing in the Grand River with the early morning mist rising and seeing the deer coming down for a drink, the ducks flying overhead and even the occasional near-silent hot air balloon drifting by. I enjoy all these things and more. These other interests make up a much smaller part of my identity, but they could have been more dominant if, for example, I had found filmmaking to be less interesting.

So let's consider what your new identity is going to be and how you'll make the transition. No matter how you stop your working life and enter your Fit retirement years, you need a plan.

The First Day After Your Last Day At Work

So, yesterday was your last day at work. Now what? Oh, I know, you have lots of projects on the go, things you started months or years ago; clean out the attic or the crawl space where even the St. Bernard won't go. Finish the needlepoint you started when Trudeau Senior was in power. Re-plant the rose bed. Paint the spare bedroom. Rotate the tires. Yep, you sure have a lot to do. That will occupy you for a while, but then what? Oh yes, you wanted to start some new hobbies: scuba diving, fly fishing, learning another language, social dancing. Have you ever tried any of these, or are these the things you just think would be fun? I'd like to suggest to you that it will be much easier for you to simply expand the time you spend on an existing hobby than to try to start one from scratch the day after you retire.

That is, if you think that social dancing looks like fun (and I can tell you that it is), then start it today. Start it in a small way — take a few lessons, find out where and when there are local public dances, get to know some people who have been dancing for a while. Learn some of the history of the dances and get involved. Perhaps you take one 1-hour lesson a week and you go to a public dance once a month. You find you really like it and you are pretty good at it. Great! Do that for a couple of years before you retire. When you retire, increase the number of public dances you attend, maybe twice a month, and take an extra lesson a week. Perhaps by the time you retire you are good enough to give lessons. This way, on the day you retire your calendar is already filled with fun stuff that you have enjoyed for years. The only difference is you are doing more of them, or doing them more often because you already know that you enjoy them. Of course I use dancing as an example, but there are tons of other examples.

The same goes for other, less physically strenuous activities, such as lecture series, concerts, or other learning events. Put your name on these mailing lists now and attend when you can. Getting excited about the speaker list will also increase your emotional readiness to stop working and change your daily life. Then, when you retire, you are already in the loop and you can attend all those lectures you missed because of work.

1,001 Things to do Before You Die

Have you noticed I haven't talked at all about a "bucket list"?[26] This is because I haven't found the need for one. I think it was a great premise for a movie, a book and merchandise; however, I think we are all far more comfortable in doing things that allow us to grow as a person. And yes, I've seen those Facebook things where people list all the stuff they've done. All the books they've read, all the films they've watched, all the cities they've visited, all the foods they've eaten. Most bucket lists I've seen appear to be a collection of "Been there, done that and here's a selfie of me in the T-shirt"; just lots of one-off experiences; notches on their guns. As I said earlier, some people subscribe to the adage that "he who dies with the most toys wins." In my opinion bucket lists amount to the same thing. I won't tell you how many countries I've visited — that's unimportant and irrelevant. But I will tell you about some of the fantastic people I've met in my travels, some of the wonderful foods I've eaten (and not so wonderful food: curried frogs, fish head soup, insects) and some of what I've learned visiting those countries.

Oh sure, sometimes I think it would be nice to visit New Zealand, for example. But I wouldn't visit just to cross it off some list. My life

[26] http://www.imdb.com/title/tt0825232/

wouldn't be unfulfilled if I died without visiting New Zealand. And I mean no slight to the Kiwis reading this — I've heard the country is very beautiful and that the people are fantastic, but you know, I say the same thing about Canada, and I will never get to every beautiful spot in Canada, nor will I ever meet every fantastic Canadian in my lifetime. I hope I don't sound blasé about this. You know I like to travel, but not to just cross something off a list.

Rather than a checklist, where I cross things off as I do them much as I do for my weekly chores around the house, I like to do things where I can develop myself, like making films, golfing (well nobody really improves at golf, do they?), gardening, dancing, and learning new languages. Will I ever be completely fluent in Spanish and so cross it off a bucket list? *¡Nunca en mi vida!* (Never in my life!). But I'm having a lot of fun learning it and meeting Spanish-speaking people and traveling in Spanish-speaking countries. Will I ever stop playing golf and cross it off my list because I'm the best in the world? Ha! For me, these things that I do on a continual basis enrich my life far more than checking items off a list.

Perhaps a bucket list works for you, and to you I say "good for you." The crucial point is to find your motivation to get up and get going every day. And perhaps there is a middle ground where you do things that allow you to grow and learn with a very short list of one-offs. Ultimately it comes down to what motivates and inspires you — what you find fulfilling. Perhaps it is something new — perhaps you'll do something you used to do but dropped to raise a family, like art or music. This can be a whole new chapter in your life of volunteerism, expanding dormant interests. Whatever it may be, you need to find something that will give purpose and meaning to your life.

Sometimes your hobbies and interests are decided for you. Your spouse decides that social dancing would be really nice and suggests that you would like it too, and you know what? You love it. A friend invites you to join a service club or social club. A friend of a friend has an extra ticket to a lecture series that you use, and find you really enjoy it and so continue with other lectures. My father, at 87, still plays golf at least three times a week, and he had been after me for years to join him. I had tried golf decades ago and found that when I did connect with the ball it usually went anywhere but where I had intended, so I immediately gave up on it. A couple of years before I retired, my wife and I were visiting dad and he had a surprise for us. He brought out a brand new set of golf clubs, not for me, but for my wife. Crafty fellow. My wife had played in a few charity tournaments with borrowed clubs, but that was all. Well, after a couple of months she was doing pretty well and invited me out. With her patience and instruction, I was doing pretty well. So I bought some used clubs. The following season I bought some new clubs and then joined a league. That wasn't in the plan for me, but there you are. Oh yes, we still play golf with dad, but certainly not three times a week.

If counting things helps to create a plan for yourself, try counting the number of people you have helped in your life. While I don't see any need in telling you the number of countries I've visited, I am incredibly proud to say that as I write this I have donated blood 38 times and have scheduled number 39. When my mom was diagnosed with leukemia, her doctor started her on blood transfusions to attempt to get her healthy enough to start chemotherapy. While she never became healthy enough for the chemo, all those blood donations kept her alive for a few extra weeks so she could enjoy her family just a little longer. After she died, I thought about all those people who never knew my mom and never would but had donated blood so that someone, anyone, Irma Pell, could spend a few more weeks with her family. I started donating just after she died; it was late in life, but I started. As some blood can be used for multiple people, that's at least 38 people I've helped. Perhaps I've even helped you or someone you love.

As a professional trainer, I've trained hundreds of university students and thousands of adults to become better programmers and software users and administrators. As a volunteer, I've helped countless people less fortunate than myself. Counting these things is far more important to me than the number of movies I've seen or beers I've sampled. Well, okay, perhaps there is some merit in sampling 1,001 beers.

Making The World A Better Place

If you haven't been "giving back" or "paying it forward" (or whatever phrase people are using these days), perhaps it is time to consider volunteering. I can give you all kinds of reasons for doing this and tell you how great it feels to do good things, but you have to experience it to really know. Perhaps you think you have little to offer as a volunteer — you don't know how to change a lightbulb let alone build a house, you never liked English grammar so don't want to teach English as a second language to immigrants making a new life here, and you've always had a black thumb when it comes to gardening so volunteering with the horticultural society is out. Never fear — there are lots of things you can do that require no special skills other than the desire to help others. You might also consider using your former professional skills for the organization where you volunteer.

> Caution! Be careful that you don't end up doing your old job and not getting paid for it. I know a fellow who worked as a chartered accountant for many, many years. When he retired, he joined a service club, and they immediately made him the treasurer. He did this for a couple of years but eventually quit the club as he felt he was just doing his regular work without pay. He is very happy in another service club doing lots of things that are not directly related to money.

The only difficulty with volunteering that you may have is deciding where to volunteer, as there are hundreds of opportunities for you. Here are just a few:

- Hospital auxiliary
- Blood donor clinic — you can donate blood but also volunteer to give out juice and cookies to donors

- Humane Society
- Food Bank
- Library
- Community recreation centre
- Multicultural groups
- Ethnic groups
- The Canadian Legion
- Service Clubs

The list goes on and on. Your local newspaper may occasionally publish a list of organizations looking for volunteers. There are volunteer fairs you can attend. You can even ask at your city hall or local volunteer centre.

I want to put in a special plug for service clubs. You are reading this book, which means you are thinking of retirement, which means that you believe you will be fit to retire. This also means that you might have the time to volunteer in your community right now and expand that time when you retire. For me, this is the most rewarding way to spend my time, helping others. Many service clubs meet regularly when they are not involved in a project and so keep their members active and engaged. I can't urge you strongly enough to give a couple of hours of your time a week. It's fun, you meet great, like-minded people and you do good stuff in your community. When you retire, you can easily increase the time you give to the level that

Rotary

suits you.

I am a Rotarian (a member of the Rotary International organization). We do wonderful work locally and around the world. One aspect of

Rotary that makes it something for you to investigate is that there are Rotary clubs in almost every city in almost every country in the world. If you are planning on traveling when you retire, imagine going to some distant place and walking into a Rotary meeting there and having 40 or 50 instant friends. No kidding — it really is like that. Many of them will be happy to tell you about their town or city, and some may even show you around. And by the same token, when Rotarians from distant places visit your home club, you'll welcome them in the same manner as you are welcomed there. It is a wonderful way to make international friends.

I have attended Rotary meetings all over the world and in many languages that I don't understand, but I've always been welcome. Let me share just one example. I was training customers in Bangalore, India and found that there was a Rotary club not far from my hotel that met for dinner. I love Indian food and so was really looking forward to this. I was welcomed like a friend and introduced as a respected guest from Canada. Club members are usually billed for their meals, and guests are asked to pay at the door, which I did. I learned quite a bit about the club during the meeting and met some great people, but dinner was never served. When the meeting wrapped up, I asked about dinner, and there was a bit of embarrassment that no one had told me that they all pay for their dinner, but rather than spending the money on food for themselves, they spend the money on a breakfast program for local school children whose parents can't afford to feed them breakfast. I was so impressed with this that I paid twice and went back to my hotel for a late dinner.

But again, don't wait until you retire, find a Rotary club or similar group in your area and contact them. They will be warm and welcoming and will invite you to a meeting (no obligation to check them out) so you can meet the members and see for yourself.

But I Really Don't Know What I Want To Do When I Grow Up

"Okay, Howard, this is all well and good for you. You seem to have found some things that really satisfy and fulfil you, but I honestly don't know what I want to do with myself."

Since starting this book and speaking with a lot of people about what they want to do when they retire, I'm surprised at the number of people who tell me this. I'm not 100% sure, but I believe that some of this stems from over-choice. We live in a time when there are so many opportunities to do things, so many good causes to get involved in, so many special interest groups asking us to participate, that it is easy to get overwhelmed. Unfortunately for many, the fallback position is to do none of them out of sheer exhaustion at just trying to understand them all. Let's see if we can narrow the field a little.

All your working life you may have used your intellectual muscles or your leadership muscles, and now is the time to concentrate on your artistic muscles. Or perhaps it is vice versa; your art, music, acting etc. was your life for the past 30+ years and now it is time to do something completely different. Perhaps you've been so busy with work-related and family-related stuff you've not spent any time on developing your own interests.

This will take a little reflection on your part, but try to think back to when you were a teenager. You were very passionate about many things. You were going to save the world, or at least make it a better place. You got really excited about music and art. You loved to read literature, perhaps even poetry. You may have even tried your hand at writing poetry. You didn't have much money, but what money you had, you spent on your car, or your stereo, or your books. You sewed, did crafts, built radios, model cars, trains, airplanes. Played the piano or guitar. What was it that really "turned you on?" Can you identify one or two things that you really enjoyed? Now, why did you give them up? You got a really good job that you loved, you got married and "settled down", started a family. Somehow there just wasn't enough time in the day, and the guitar stayed in its case and gathered dust. You sold your car and bought a mini-van for the kids and the St. Bernard. Do you see where I'm going? Of course, you sold the guitar years ago, but the pawnshops are bursting with used guitars. There are hundreds of "meet up" groups where people can talk about, and enjoy, their passion, be it guitars, Spanish, cooking or fishing: try www.meetup.com and you'll be amazed.

> Hot Damn! I just went to www.meetup.com and searched for "Kitchener" (where I live) and "film" (one of my hobbies) and found five meetups. I have to check them out.

Okay, you were young and didn't know what you wanted. Or perhaps you got caught up in the 60s "drugs, sex and rock and roll," which seemed to me like a pretty good way to spend my youth. But still, you had values, you cared about things deeply. Then as you aged you found yourself drawn to things at work, some movies and books made a real impression on you, and so did some people. Remember the guy who coached hockey, the woman who was a Snowy Owl with Brownies, the bowling league you joined one winter? Remember the woman who had three kids and six grandchildren and couldn't wait to retire so she could be a full-time grandma? Do you remember thinking "Wow, I'd really like to do that when I retire?" You still have passions. You are appalled by child abuse, animal abuse. The idea of eco-tourism really excites you.

Building schools in underdeveloped countries sounds like a wonderful use of your time. Coaching children's soccer sounds like it could be a real joy.

Here is a short exercise for you: Fill in the table below with things you think of right now. Don't ponder it too much, but be honest with yourself.

Notice the Reward column, which will be a big indicator to you of whether you'd like to do the activity again. And of course, feel free to add new activities and interests to the table, things you think you'll enjoy and will give you the kind of reward you want.

There isn't much I remember about public school, but I do recall a day when our teacher brought in a guest who asked us to write a story. The story was to be instructions on how to do something. We could pick anything we wanted, but I recall we were given examples. I vividly remember choosing to write about how to change a flat tire. I wrote in painful detail, step-by-step instructions on how to loosen the wheel nuts before you jack up the car, where to find the spare tire, and on and on. I wanted to show people how to do it. I completely forgot about this until I was in the second year of my undergraduate program, and got a job as a T.A. (Teachers' Assistant) and I fell in love with teaching. The prof I was working for liked heli-skiing in Whistler, B.C. and frequently had me deliver his lectures. My public school essay came back to me, and I knew I'd found my

Interest/ Activity	**What I liked about it**	**What I disliked about it**	**Reward**	**Would I do it again**
Play Guitar	Creative, artistic	Fingers hurt	Nice to entertain people	Yes
Coach Little League	I love children	I dislike parents	Helped children	No
Part-time tax advisor	Named my own hours	A lot of stress	$$$	Yes

profession: helping others to learn. Since then, I've loved to learn and then share what I've learned with my students. And that love of learning and sharing has carried over into my retirement through my volunteer work and in some of the videos that I make. Many years ago my wife gave me a wall plaque that reads:

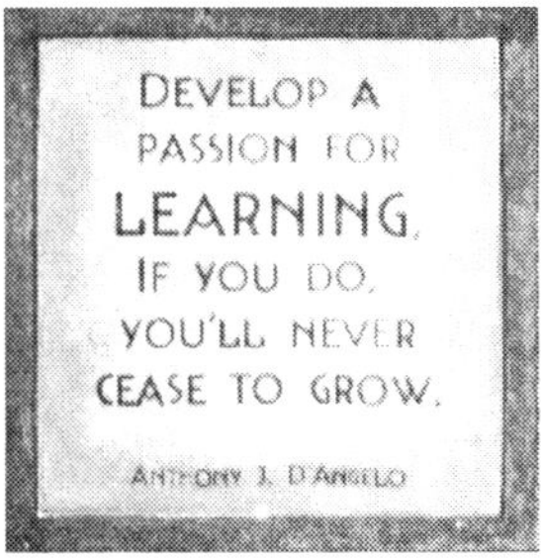

Develop a passion for learning. If you do, you'll never cease to grow.
Anthony J. D'Angelo

I see it every time I sit down at my desk.

So take some time to think about what really excited and motivated you in your youth and perhaps through your early adulthood. Things that you had to put on the back burner while your family and employer made demands on your time. For the most part, those demands are now gone, and perhaps it is time to go to the back burner to see what's still simmering there after all these years.

The First Year After Your Last Day At Work

Just one word of advice concerning making *unplanned* changes in your life during the first year of retirement:
Don't!

You've made a plan, so stick with it.

Retirement is a change. A big change. And like all change it is stressful.

"Huh? What do you mean, stressful? I'm going to relax — where's the stress in that?"

To begin with, as I mentioned before, you are no longer the same person, you have changed, you are no longer a manager, a chef, a police officer, a teacher, an administrator. Oh sure, you feel the same, but your friends and co-workers (former co-workers now) see you differently, and perhaps with envy. You have escaped, moved on; you are no longer one of them but the lucky dog who doesn't care about the office anymore. You now have a new St. Bernard puppy. You don't care about the office gossip: who is sleeping with whom, or that the latest product release is taking the market by storm, or which customer complained yesterday about something that should have been fixed last year. You really aren't interested in how great the new department head is; or what the most hated manager in the plant, the one they call the human hemorrhoid, said to the new receptionist. In fact, you've never even met the new receptionist.

Retirement is a big change, and it can be stressful enough — don't add to it by making other big changes in your life right away. I remember reading Peter Hanson's *The Joy of Stress* many years ago; he explained how even "good" events were stressful, and retirement is a really good event.

You will find that after a month or two, should you happen by the office or the plant for a visit, your former co-workers are happy to see you, of course, and want to hear how retirement is treating you, but they have their work to do and can't really hang out with you in the middle of the day. Or if you meet them after hours for dinner or a drink, you will find that they have new issues to discuss that you know nothing about. Or even worse, they will have the same issues you were dealing with a year ago and they are still not resolved.

So this will be stressful for you. Don't add to your stress level.

No unplanned changes, period.

Don't:

- sell your house or buy a house unless you have carefully planned for this
- move from one apartment to another
- get divorced
- get married
- make any large unplanned expenditures like buying a boat or cottage

Do:

- make plans for those events if you are considering them

So try to use your first year of retirement as an easing-in period. Take your time, see how things go, revisit the plans you made the previous year(s), and see how you feel about them now. Do you really want a boat, or would you be just as happy renting a boat when you want? Do you really want to move just yet, or conversely, do you really want to stay in your house when your plan said you were going to sell and move into a nice apartment? Try to keep with your plan, but also feel free to revise your plan after the first year or so.

So let's return to Tony Robbin's Six Human Needs and see how they fit here:

1. **Certainty**: assurance you can avoid pain and gain pleasure
   – Along with your financial and physical fitness, your emotional fitness will help with avoiding pain and gaining pleasure by preparing yourself mentally for this.
2. **Uncertainty/Variety**: the need for the unknown, change, new stimuli
   – By being emotionally fit and ready to take on new challenges, and by being ready to explore and ready for new experiences, we keep our minds sharp and active. The alternative is 10 hours a day of TV drivel.
3. **Significance**: feeling unique, important, special or needed
   – There are so many things that you as an emotionally fit person will want to engage in that you will satisfy this need with ease. You'll find yourself doing things you never thought you'd do, with people you never thought you'd meet.
4. **Connection/Love**: a strong feeling of closeness or union with someone or something
   – Speaking of meeting people, you're going to meet some great people as you become more active outside your work environment. You'll be volunteering more, and you'll be going to more social events (lectures, dances, films, book clubs). You won't feel the loss of your "work family" if you develop other connections.
5. **Growth**: an expansion of capacity, capability or understanding
   – I've been an adult educator most of my career, and I love to learn and then share what I've learned. But Growth also applies to you physically - don't forget I still have that treadmill available.
6. **Contribution**: a sense of service and focus on helping, giving to and supporting others.

– You know all about my love for Rotary. There are so many opportunities for you to volunteer that you only need to read your local paper.

"Crisis? What Crisis?"

Is there such a thing as a midlife crisis? Some say yes and some say no. I'm not an expert and I can only tell you what I've read and what I've experienced. From what I've read, it seems that the experts are divided on whether this is a real and treatable condition or if it is just another phase of life. That is, if I understand correctly, some feel that it can be classified along with other changes of life such as puberty. For some it is very dramatic, while for others it is a minor event. For people undergoing a major change, I'm sure it is real enough. The reason I raise this issue is that it seems to occur sometime after your 40th birthday, and so with people retiring younger all the time, it may happen to you, it may have already happened, or it may be just around the corner.

There seem to be a number of symptoms, both physical and emotional, and perhaps some of the physical ones trigger the emotional ones. It appears that people become unhappy or dissatisfied with their career, their marriage or their health. As we discussed earlier, their body changes shape and loses tone, their eyesight, hearing, sense of smell all change. And let's face it — being retired means we have fewer years ahead of us than behind us. All of these factors can cause emotional reactions. External factors happen as well: Some become a grandparent, and people they know, including their parents, die.

From what I've read, symptoms include: boredom, exhaustion, self-doubt, irritability, drinking, drugs, and change in sexual desire, including extra-marital affairs. They become confused as to what they really want to do with the rest of their life, and in some cases just want to run away and hide. Like most emotional issues, the key to resolving it is to recognize it and accept it for what it is. Some people seem to be able to shake it off quite easily, while others require the help of a professional. Frequently, it is spotted by those close to you far sooner than by yourself, so pay attention when someone you know questions your moods or asks you if everything is okay.

What about me? When I turned 40 I had the following brief conversation with my wife:

Me: "I think I'll buy a motorcycle or maybe a sports car."
She: "Oh! What kind of sports car will you get?"

She was so subtle. I bought a beautiful, new, white Acura Integra, just big enough for two. I had that car for 20 years. It was still mechanically perfect, but the body was so rotten that it was impossible to keep patching it. So I replaced it with a very gently used, green Mazda Miata (*zoom, zoom*). The Integra was a wonderful car to drive, very comfortable, with an almost luxury feel. The Miata, on the other hand, drives more like my old MGB; close to the ground, very fast, very hard suspension that allows for incredible cornering — you get the idea. So no motorcycle. However, driving my Miata around town while most men my age are driving their vans and SUVs does give me the feeling that I'm younger than my 62 years.

Was that my "crisis?" Perhaps not; I changed jobs just after my 40th and also kept the job for 20 years. Now, a year after my retirement, I did discover a few of the symptoms mentioned above but was able to identify them and talk them through with my wife. She's wonderful.

My thoughts are that if you've already had your crisis and have dealt with it, then bravo. If you haven't had one yet, then be on the lookout for it, and I hope it never happens to you. But if it does, I hope you identify it quickly and deal with it quickly and wisely. As I said above, don't make any sudden changes in your life that you haven't planned for. Those unplanned changes may just be the result of a delayed "mid-life" crisis.

Thy Will Be Done

I've saved this section on legal documents for this chapter on emotional fitness because by creating these documents you will gain a lot of peace of mind knowing that these are taken care of and that you don't need to worry about them.

What is a will? While you are alive, you make the decisions about your estate (all your worldly possessions). For example, if you want to pay for your son to stay in university for yet another degree, you decide (it is your decision, your wish, your **will**), that some money from your bank account is transferred into his account, or to the university's. While you are alive, you make your **will** known by your actions — deposit money into your son's university's account. After you die, someone else will see that your **will** is carried out by making that deposit. A legal, written will is a document that indicates all your final decisions (final wishes, final will) after you are dead regarding what happens to all your stuff: money, house, books, ugly figurine that Aunt Katherine gave you, the St. Bernard that is no longer a puppy. And it reflects your decisions as if you are still alive. Plain and simple, you must have one, and it must be done with the help of a lawyer. If you don't have a will, then the government steps in, and like everything else, you want to avoid government interference as much as possible.

Don't cheap out on this unless you really don't like the person you've asked to be your executor. That is, yes, lawyers are expensive (see Professional Help, below), but saving a few bucks by writing your will on the back of an old water bill will cost your estate a lot more in the long run and will cause a lot of grief for your executor. A lawyer will ensure that your will is legally correct and will help you arrange your affairs to make disposing of your estate according to your will as easy as possible for your executor. And if you are asked to be an executor and the person asking you doesn't have a will, or if that will is written on a cocktail napkin in what appears to be blue Curacao, then run, don't walk, away.

My parents used those wills you buy from stationery stores for $1.99 ($1.99 when they bought them). When my mother passed away, my lawyer was rather dubious about her will, but as my dad was still living, everything went to him. I'm sure that for very, very simple wills, these stationery store wills might be okay; however, as the world gets more and more complex (and family dynamics do too),

I'd advise against them. Are you legally separated or divorced? Are you single, common-law or legally married? Do you have children? step-children? Do you own multiple properties? All these things make for complexity in settling your estate. Even a short consultation with a lawyer will be worth the fee to tell you how complex settling your estate *could* be without a proper will.

After my mother died, I looked at my father's will (the $1.99 one) and couldn't make out the witness's signature. I asked him who it was. It took some deep thought on his part, but it turns out it was one of his buddies that he meets at Tim's, but he couldn't recall the guy's last name. Over dad's objections, I had my lawyer redraw his will properly. I even paid for it, as I knew he'd balk at the fee. When the time comes, I, as the executor, can take dad's will to any lawyer in Canada, and all is well from that point of view.

What is an executor? This is the person who sees to it that your will is carried out. He or she does everything you've indicated in your will and a whole lot more. Just for starters, your executor will cancel all your credit cards, report your death to multiple government agencies (Provincial Health Care, Ministry of Transportation, Canada Revenue Agency), cancel magazine and newspaper subscriptions, pay your final income tax, distribute your possessions to family members as you've indicated or as they request, sell all your stuff. The list goes on and on.

Choose this person with care; this can be a thankless task, depending on how complex your estate is and how well your family members

get along. Yes, reasonable, loving families have been known to come to blows over the distribution of the estate. Siblings refuse to talk with each other except through their lawyers. Stepchildren can argue with natural children, etc. etc. It can be a very traumatic time for everyone and, especially for the person you assign to execute your will. I had thought of including some examples of these family meltdowns here, but if you want horror stories, just ask your lawyer — I'm sure he or she has loads of them.

You obviously want an executor who is responsible, can get things done, and stands a good chance of outliving you. Your tattooed, pierced, squeegee-toting grandson who lives in a refrigerator box might not be the best choice.

Something that does not go into your will but may be just as important or even more important is your funeral arrangements and how your survivors should deal with your remains. If you have any preference at all, then you must tell someone, preferably in writing. This is not the most pleasant task, but if you have any strong feeling on the matter then you have to let someone know. On the other hand, you could just leave it to your kids or executor to decide. After all, you'll be dead, so what do you care?

Leaving Money to Charities

We all have our favourite charities, and we all give as generously as we possibly can. Many charities now offer legacy giving opportunities where you can leave part of (or your entire) estate to your favourite charities. Your lawyer can help you with this, and the charities are often happy to help as well.

You might also wish to consider purchasing life insurance and making the charity the beneficiary. Here again, your lawyer can help you, and so can your insurance agent.

Both these options may also offer tax advantages. Your insurance agent or accountant can advise you about them. This may leave more cash to distribute to the beneficiaries so that they can all buy St. Bernard puppies.

For a Few Dollars More

There are two more legal documents you need to know about, because in many ways it really does suck to get old, and you may need some assistance as you age towards geezerhood and your good health deteriorates. Knowing that you'll be cared for in the way you want, by someone you trust, is an important contributor to your emotional fitness.

Power of Attorney

A Power of Attorney (POA) is another document that your lawyer can draw up for you. It essentially gives someone else the legal right to act on your behalf when you are unable to act. Here is a very good web site from the Ontario Government[27] with some valuable information on POAs.

In Ontario there are three types of POA:

- A Continuing POA allows someone to act on your behalf for all your financial affairs.

[27] Ontario Government POA - www.attorneygeneral.jus.gov.on.ca/english/family/pgt/poakit.asp

- A Non-continuing POA is similar but does not apply if, or when, you become mentally incapacitated. Use this one only if you are away from home for extended periods of time. Like when you decide that Spanish winters are much nicer than Canadian winters.
- A POA for personal care covers your personal decisions such as where you live and healthcare decisions.

Of course we hope we never find ourselves in the situation where we have to defer to someone else because we are unable to either decide or unable to communicate our decision. In short, and to be perfectly blunt, if you should have a stroke, be in a coma, or anything else that makes it impossible for you to communicate clearly, the person with your POA will make decisions for you. Consider this to be a kind of insurance should you ever find yourself in need.

Choosing someone to be your POA is much like choosing an executor. You need to trust them to be reliable and to make the right decisions for you. So talk it over with them and ensure they know your thoughts. Better yet, write it down for them.

Living Will /Advance Directive

An advance directive is a document in which you tell (direct) others about the kinds of treatment you do and don't want; you create this document in *advance*, in case bad things happen and you are in no state to tell anybody anything (because you fell and got a head injury while walking your St. Bernard, developed dementia, are in a coma, etc.). A living will is a common type of advance directive that is separate from your last will and testament. Why do you need one?

One example is: some people don't wish to be kept alive on artificial life support if there is no hope they will recover, and a living will could direct others to act by your wishes.

There is no need to appoint someone to administer your living will — you just give it to someone you trust to produce it should the need arise, probably your executor or lawyer. But most importantly, you must tell your care providers that the document exists. It's also a really good idea to talk with your loved ones about what your living will says, because otherwise, they might try to act on your behalf based on false assumptions about what you want.

So that covers a lot of the "Certainty" issue about what will happen to you in your retirement and after your death. That should give you some peace of mind knowing that you've looked after the people you love as well as yourself.

> *"Of course, the whole point of a Doomsday Machine is lost, if you *keep* it a *secret*! Why didn't you tell the world, EH?"*
>
> Dr. Strangelove

Now that you've created all these documents it is time to tell someone about them, perhaps not the world, but someone. Better yet, put them all in one place and tell your lawyer, your executor, or both where they are, because it is all part of your peace of mind. Now imagine it is the day after you die. Someone has to do all the things you said you'd do but somehow never got around to doing, like: close almost empty bank accounts; find a buyer for your stamp collection, coin collection, doll collection, or whatever; make your funeral arrangements; and many other things. By making it easy (or at least easier) for your survivors, you can sleep easier yourself without worrying about these things. How about another list? Be as complete as you possibly can. Here's an example:

My list of important documents and things. By Howard Pell - last updated 2016 January 15

In my fireproof box / office safe / lawyer's office / old mayonnaise jar behind the furnace, you will find the following documents:

- Our wills
- Our birth certificates
- Our Social Insurance Cards
- Our marriage certificate
- Our POAs
-
-

In my wallet you'll find:

- My driver's license
- My provincial health card
- My credit cards
- My bank cards
-
-

List of all our financial information

- Our financial advisor is [name, phone, email, address]
    - – Our account number(s) is / are
- Our lawyer is [name, phone, email, address]
- At the [name, phone, email, address] bank our account(s) number(s) is / are (multiple entries, 1 per bank)
- We have a safety deposit box at [name, phone, email, address]
- Our funeral arrangements are at [name, phone, email, address]

- Our insurance agent is [name, phone, email, address] and policy number(s) is/are
-
-

List of all my passwords

- Facebook
- Google
- Yahoo
- LinkedIn
- iTunes store
- At the [name, phone, email, address] bank our password(s) is/are
- Credit card
-
-

And don't forget to update this list when things change. Or perhaps a better idea is to review everything on a special day that you'll remember: your anniversary, your birthday, the St. Bernard's birthday. And of course, let your executor know you've updated everything and give them a copy or details on locating it.

Professional Help

We've talked about legal, financial and tax professionals. There is another category to consider.

> Retirement is the opportunity for you to become whoever you want to be; but you need to figure that out first and then plan for it.

Personal coaches, also known as life coaches, can help you come to terms with who you are and where you'd like to be. Many people have a pretty good handle on this already — or at least they did in their working life, and now comes the big change. Personal coaches can help you understand all these issues we've been talking about and can help you determine your new identity.

You've heard me say this already, but it bears repeating. I'm not a professional life coach, and so if I was feeling a little at sea with the whole idea of retirement, I would definitely hire one to help me out. For many new retirees, it isn't that there is nothing that really interests them, it is more the case that there are just too many things that interest them, and picking just one, two or even seven would mean that they might miss out on all the others that they didn't pick. This is where a life coach can really help you determine where to focus your energies.

But just like other professionals I've spoken about, don't just pick a coach from the phone book. Ask your friends, family, co-workers, etc. who they use. Then interview them: What standard services do they provide? What extras can they provide? How do they tailor their advice to you? And do you like them as a person? Do you respect them? Do you think you will listen to their advice and follow it? If not, this isn't the coach for you — find someone else.

Choosing a lawyer is slightly different. This need not be a long-term relationship, but it can be. Your will, once drawn up, will rarely need revision, typically only due to deaths, births, marriages and divorces.

Your lawyer will ensure you don't do anything that would slow down the process of settling your estate. Consider the example I gave earlier of you leaving $1,000 to your firstborn and the remainder to the second born. What happens if all that's left in the estate is $900? Does your executor now owe your firstborn $100 out of their pocket? Again, ask around for recommendations. Once again, I strongly recommend that you have a lawyer draw up this very important document.

Did I Hear You Correctly?

I was very fortunate: My sister-in-law gave me a book on retirement many, many years ago that briefly mentioned preparing yourself emotionally, and it struck me that that brief mention was the best bit of advice in the entire book. Alas, the book went to one of the charity used-book sales years ago, but I took that advice to heart, and I'm glad I did. I had only a few reference points to observe retirees. The first few years were very difficult for my father-in-law (and, by extension, my mother-in-law) as he just didn't know what to do with himself. He was a high-school teacher and after retiring did a bit of supply teaching, but he knew he had to find something else quickly. He finally got his sea legs and enjoyed a long and productive, fit retirement and then a mercifully very short Geezerhood.

Supply teaching = Substitute teaching

My father, on the other hand, always owned his own business. He eased into his retirement by selling his business and taking a part-time job as a pharmacist's assistant, something completely new to him. He'd work a few days a week and occasionally an entire week to cover for someone on vacation. It was sometimes a fine line to walk when they needed him almost full-time for weeks on end, as he didn't want to lose the job if he said "no" but didn't want to work that much if he said "yes." But he loved going to work. He loved talking with the customers and the staff. Eventually he quit, and today he spends most of his time on the golf course.

Your emotional fitness is very closely tied to your physical fitness. Be prepared and know your limitations. If you can swing this, try to ease your way into retirement — part-time employment really worked for me. One of the most important things you can do is to create an exit plan for yourself, and don't forget to have a contingency plan if your exit plan can't be met.

If you have a partner (and children), then you need to include him/her/them in all of your retirement plans. Take your time and talk about this, then talk some more, and then talk even more. And be prepared to adjust to your partner's life stage as well.

Don't forget that retirement is a big change, starting with a change in your identity, as you will no longer be the person you were when you were working. Plan and prepare for this. Also, plan for filling 40+ hours a week. Perhaps volunteering will be your answer, but be sure to try a variety of things to keep you busy.

So as we've seen, emotional fitness is incredibly important to your success as a fit retiree. Take some time and think of this. Develop a plan; don't be afraid to update and modify it as you go, but develop that plan.

References and Worksheets

Disclaimer: I am listing the following URLs because these are the first ones I found on the Internet; I know you'll find lots more. I am not recommending them — I am only pointing out that there are a great many of these available. I take no responsibility for your success (or lack of success) with any of the following.

By the way, all of the following URLs were working when we went to print. As we all know, web pages are always being updated and changed, and so some of these links may not be active by the time you read this book. I will try to keep this list updated on my website www.howardpell.ca.

Links To Life Coaches

As you might expect, life coaches typically work in their local area. I live in Kitchener, Ontario, so for me to give you a list of life coaches here won't help you very much if you live in Calgary. I think the best thing for you to do is ask around. Check with friends and family to see if they can recommend someone.

Documents You Have

Keeping these documents close to hand is not really necessary. May I suggest that you keep a copy and that your lawyer keep the originals? In that way, when the time comes that you need them (or your executor needs them), you don't have to go hunting for them — just phone your lawyer.

- ☐ Your will
- ☐ Partner's will
- ☐ Your Powers of Attorney
- ☐ Your partner's Powers of Attorney
- ☐ If you are the executor for other people — their will(s) and power(s) of attorney
- ☐ Insurance policies
- ☐ Living will
- ☐ Not really a document, but have you indicated to your lawyer who your executor is?
- ☐ Have you told someone what funeral arrangements you want?
- ☐ A list of important numbers and names - Bank Accounts, Life Insurance, Passwords, Lawyer, Financial Advisor(s)

Work Exit Plan

This need not be overly complex, as you saw with mine. You can start with a simple plan and add to it as you think of more details, but unless you feel the real need for complexity, Keep It Simple.

Goal - To retire from paid employment	
Best case scenario -	
2nd best case scenario -	
3rd best case scenario -	
Add more here if you need	
Worst case scenario -	

Volunteering And Keeping Busy

Here are just a few links that might give you some ideas of what you might like to do in your retirement.

Rotary International
https://www.rotary.org/

Canadian Blood Services
https://www.blood.ca/

Road Scholar - Elderhostel
http://www.roadscholar.org/n/country/country.aspx?regioncode=canada

MOOC (Massively Open Online Courses)
https://www.mooc-list.com/

Volunteer Canada
http://volunteer.ca/

CHAPTER FIVE

You Are Fit, Fit, Fit

Each of our days is numbered without price, and never to return. When we know that our time is limited, it becomes so much more precious. The drive to achieve, to create, to leave behind something that says "I was here", "I mattered", it becomes so much stronger.

K.R. Ravindran, 2015-16 President Rotary International

Introduction

Time to look at a couple of case studies. I know there is no such thing as the "average" case, and so I won't try. However, whenever I see those case studies in the newspapers (you know, the ones with their faces covered), I always cringe at the huge amount of wealth these people have. Rather, I want to look at people who are a bit closer to the average and who, I hope, are the ones reading this book. Having said this, we must note that you are an expert on you. Everyone is different, and although there are probably thousands of people who will retire on the same day that you retire, you are unique. Recognizing your uniqueness allows me to also reiterate the need for professional assistance. That is, no matter how much I would like my book to be the only one you'll ever need, I recognize that it can't be everything to everyone. Your successful retirement will depend on you, what you learn from articles and books like this one, as well as your support group.

Once we look at the case studies, I want to do a short review of my own circumstances, one year after retiring — how do I feel, were there any surprises, have I done anything differently from what I planned? Well, yes, I wrote a book.

I hope this book has been useful to you and has given you some ideas that you hadn't thought about. I hope you can take these ideas to heart and that you get yourself Fit, Fit and Fit.

Setting Your Retirement Date

We have seen that there are three primary factors in retiring and that they all take their place in calculating the date you will retire. Ideally you will retire when:

1. you are financially fit enough to do what you want to do
2. you are physically fit enough to do what you want to do
3. you are emotionally fit enough to do what you want to do

Think of this as a three-way horse race to decide when you can retire. Or perhaps a three-way St. Bernard race.

So now you have a pretty good idea of when you'll retire — as soon as all three of your St. Bernards cross the finish line. Of course it would be pure kismet if all three cross the finish line on the same day or even in the same month, but I think it is safe to say that your goal is to get them "close enough" for you to announce your retirement date. If you are like I was, with a long history at my employer, you may wish to give them a lot of notice. I had been working for the same company for 20 years and I thought it only fair that I give them six months notice, so it required a bit of planning on my part.

If I had to choose, I'd say that the most important fitness to acquire before retiring is your emotional fitness. Get yourself mentally ready, make your plans, and get your St. Bernards in a row for keeping yourself busy. Once you have that in place, you will be ready when your financial horse (talk about mixing metaphors) crosses the finish line. Of course, there really will never come a day when you would consider yourself perfectly financially, physically or emotionally fit although there will come a time when you are "fit enough."

Setting the date can be scary, especially if you're the type of person who likes to keep your word. When you say you're going to do something, you really do it, and you do it when you said you would. Once you start telling people you've set your retirement date, you want to keep your word, especially to your employer. Once Human Resources starts the wheel in motion, there is no turning back. Oh sure, lots of people have retired multiple times — Lance Armstrong, George Foreman, Sugar Ray Leonard, Roger Clemens, Brett Favre, Michael Jordan — the list goes on and on, and of course we can also add those people who "retire" but then go right back to their same job as a "consultant." But for the rest of us mere mortals, it is nice to do it just once. So take your time making your plans and getting yourself emotionally ready for the big day. There are so many changes just before you retire that you really want to start your planning at least 8 to 10 months before the big day.

"Help Me Rhonda", Peggy, Henry, Alfie ...

Before you do set the date, take the time to get help; talk with your support group. Everybody has them. Who are these people? For me, the primary person in my support group is my wife, but I recognize that not everyone has a partner.

I know a lot of people who are single. They are single for a variety of reasons; most of the reasons seem to be "D"-words: divorce, death, dearth of suitable partners. I only bring this up because I want to assure my single readers that having a partner is not a pre-requisite to becoming Fit, Fit, Fit for retirement. In fact, for some, it may make things simpler.

Let's look at all three fitnesses from the single person's point of view:

Financial fitness - well, of course, you are perfectly capable of building your nest egg without a partner. Doing this on one salary might take longer than on two salaries, but then again, if one partner earns considerably less than the other, then it might actually take longer for two people to build a nest egg fit for two.

Physical fitness - While a partner can help motivate you to eat well and exercise, it is ultimately your decision and your body that you are looking after. So having a partner has no real bearing on your ability to become physically fit if you are self-motivated. Of course, the right partner will motivate you and encourage you to get and keep fit, but having the wrong partner can, in some cases, be a real detriment too. In some cases, a partner can assist with your care when, and if, you become physically infirm, especially if it isn't too physically demanding. But as a single person, you will need to arrange for assistance the moment you begin to need it. For example, should I become unable to prepare our meals, my wife may still be able to do this. A single person would need to arrange for someone to prepare meals for them.

Emotional fitness - As with physical fitness, emotional fitness deals exclusively with you. Yes, a partner can help you make the decisions you need to make; but, a partner isn't necessary, especially if your

partner is the wrong partner or is at a different stage, as we saw in the chapter on emotional fitness.

By definition, a single person doesn't have a spouse or partner in their support group; however, there are lots of others in your support group to speak with, and I'll deal with them shortly.

Now that we've spoken of those people who are flying solo, we turn our attention to those who have a spouse or partner. To begin with, it is critical that you both agree on the big date. If you have your heart set on a certain date, but your partner thinks it is too early or is uncomfortable about it, your retirement is not going to get off to a great start. Where do you need to agree? As I just mentioned, your physical fitness deals exclusively with you, but your partner will typically share in your emotional and financial fitness, so they need to be as ready as you are. That is, you both need to be emotionally fit for *your* retirement on the day that you retire. Get to the point where you have both done the planning and agree with the date you have set for your retirement. That's the singular "you" who is retiring — your partner may already be retired or may not wish to retire for some time, but you both need to be comfortable when just you are to retire. Lastly, you both need to feel that you are financially fit for you to retire. This may mean one of three things:

1. Your partner has retired already, and you are now financially fit enough for you to retire

2. You are financially fit for both of you to retire on the chosen date
3. You both agree that you can retire now and that your partner will keep working until both of you are financially fit for him/her to retire.

Once you are both comfortable with the decision to retire, and here I welcome back the single readers, you should speak with the rest of your support group:

- Financial advisor - are you financially fit to meet your goals?
- Lawyer - Have you made your will(s) and POAs? Have you chosen your executor(s), etc.?
- Accountant - how are your taxes looking? All paid up? Canada Revenue Agency isn't looking for you?

Canada Revenue Agency = Internal Revenue Service

- Fitness coach - are you on track to achieving your physical fitness?
- Doctor - are you managing your health?
- Dentist - are there dental issues you could do now that your new insurance may not cover?
- Your direct manager, and if appropriate, your manager's manager - how much notice do they need? Can they let you ease into your retirement?
- The rest of your family, your children, siblings and parents if they are still alive - Are there any family issues that you need to address before you retire? During your retirement?
- And anyone else you want to have a say - For example, you will have to arrange your own insurance, and that may affect

how often you visit your dentist and optometrist once you retire. In the run-up to your retirement your dentist may recommend you get some dental work done that your employer's insurance will pay for. After your retirement, your insurance may not cover everything, and your dentist may be able to offer you a small discount for your loyalty over the years when your employer's insurance paid the full shot.

All these people will help you confirm that the date you have chosen is realistic and within the realm of possibilities. As I mentioned before, once you set your date and start telling people about it, stick to it as much as you can. Of course, situations arise that may set you back in any one of your fitnesses, but if you've done your planning, you should be on target.

A Few Case Studies For Good Measure

Case Study #1 - Lucy and Charlie

Background:
Lucy - 40, undergraduate degree, administrator in the medical industry, no company pension.
Charlie - 40, high school, some college, contract administrator for government agency, no company pension.
Two children, one 13 years old by previous marriage, one 3 years old.

1. Financial Fitness:
Combined annual income = $100,000
Savings = $0

Home = renting
Debt: Car loan = $4,000
Credit cards = $6,000

Life expectancy:
Lucy - 85
Charlie - 80

Years until Charlie retires at 60 = 20

For Charlie

A	Charlie's Life Expectancy Guesstimate	80 Years
B	Charlie's Retirement Age	60 Years
C	Subtract (A - B) — This is the number of years Charlie will live without working	20 Years
D	Charlie and Lucy's Current Salary	$100,000
E	Multiply (C * D) — This is how much Charlie and Lucy will need to save.	$2,000,000

Of course this is far too simplistic, as it doesn't take into consideration the growth of their savings over the next 20 years, so we take a look at one of the many on-line calculators. Given the following:

Current Inflation Rate: 1%
Current return on investments: 8%

The calculator I tried with this data shows that by Charlie's 60th birthday, Charlie and Lucy will need $1,600,000. That's considerably less than my rough calculation above even if we add in government pensions. But they haven't started saving yet. If they can manage to save $1,000 a month, every month, then the same calculator suggests that by the time Charlie turns 60 they will have $660,000 saved; however, they are short of their retirement goal by $936,000. What to do? Now the fun of calculators happens; we play with the numbers. If we change Charlie's retirement age from 60 to 70, then they will have saved $1,715,000 and are only short $53,500. They saved almost a million dollars more by Charlie working an extra 10 years. And will they still need the same? Of course not, as they are 10 years older and 10 years closer to the day they won't need any money at all.

And so Charlie and Lucy go back to Chapter 2 of this book and review the options I outlined there as to how they are going to get financially fit for their retirement. Do they retire later? Do they get higher paying jobs? Do they live a simpler retired life?

2. Physical Fitness:

Both currently have gym memberships and work out regularly. Neither has a fitness coach, but they have good experience with gym equipment and are "at home" in the gym. Both are fit and close to their optimum weight. Even if they don't maintain their regular exercise routine for the next 25 years, they have a good base and can skip the gym every now and again. So I'd say "yes" they are probably physically fit enough to retire as long as they maintain their physical fitness routine. Of course, it all depends on what activities they want to pursue in retirement, but they are on the right track.

3. Emotional Fitness:

They are both very caught up in raising their children, and when they do have time to themselves, they spend it with each other and with their friends. It is this time in their life when they put aside those hobbies and pastimes that they will want to get back to once the 3-year old leaves home for university. It is also time for them to start thinking about what they will do when the kids leave home. The 13-year-old will start university in 5 years and the 3-year-old in 15 years. It isn't too early to start planning for the time Charlie and Lucy are by themselves.

Summary
Charlie and Lucy have some considerable planning to do for their financial fitness as well as their emotional fitness, but great news about their physical fitness.

Case Study #2 - Sally

Background:
Sally - 50, single mom, high school, some university, administrator in the hospitality industry, no company pension.
Two children, one 23 years old with 2 children, one 13 years old still living at home.
One St. Bernard, 8 years old.

1. Financial Fitness:
Annual income = $50,000
Annual child support from ex = $15,000 - Sally knows this will run out soon and has already lined up a tenant to rent her son's room when he leaves home.
Savings = $50,000
Home equity = $150,000

Debt: Credit cards = $6,000
Mortgage = $100,000

Life expectancy: 85

Years to retire at 65 = 15

For Sally

A	Sally's Life Expectancy Guesstimate	85 Years
B	Sally's Retirement Age	65 Years
C	Subtract (A - B) — This is the number of years Sally will live without working	20 Years
D	Sally's Current Salary	$50,000
E	Multiply (C * D) — This is how much Sally will need to save.	$1,000,000

Current Inflation Rate: 1%
Current return on investments: 8%

The calculator I tried with this data shows that by age 65 Sally will need $571,000 to retire. Again, that's considerably less than my rough calculation above. If she can manage to save $500 a month, every month, then the same calculator suggests that by the time Sally turns 65 she will have $348,000 saved, but she is still short of her retirement goal by $223,000. Again, we play with the numbers. If we change Sally's retirement age from 65 to 70, then she will have saved $563,000 and would only be short $11,500. Pretty close. But you've been observant and you say, "what about her house?" Yes, I did ignore it. With luck, the Canadian housing crash due to happen "next year" (or so the experts have been predicting to happen for the past 20 years) holds off, and Sally can cash in her house to add to her savings. Let's say she can sell her house at age 65 for $300,000 and that a nice apartment costs her $2,000 a month; then that $300,000 will pay for her rent for 12.5 years (until she is 77), with the assumption she gets zero growth on her $300,000. All the while, she isn't touching her savings, and they are growing a bit faster as she is now paying rent from the money she got for her house.

So while retirement at 65 may not be financially feasible for Sally, retirement at 70 should be. Again, she goes back to the options I laid out in Chapter 2 to see where she can make changes to ensure she retires when and how she wants.

2. Physical Fitness:
Sally is one of those people who are very lean even though they do not go to a gym; however, her fitness is not necessarily what it could be. Her work requires her to be on her feet a good deal of the time, but that doesn't do very much for her cardio or her upper body muscles. A gym membership is quite cheap and would allow her to work on these other aspects of her physical health that she doesn't already get, such as balance and strength. Even hiring a coach for 6 months would go a long way to help her get familiar with all the gym equipment so she can use it with confidence. Her coach can also recommend exercises for her once she is on her own.

3. Emotional Fitness:
Sally is nearing the time when her 13-year-old will leave home for university (5 years). She is active in her local townhouse community with helping the elderly. She is also becoming more active with her service club but can't dedicate a lot of time to it just yet. She has a number of hobbies when she is not driving her 13-year-old to sports and music lessons or helping with homework. So her emotional fitness is off to a good start. Once her 13-year-old is more independent, she can return to her hobbies that she dropped to have children, and she can expand on her other pastimes.

Planning Timeline

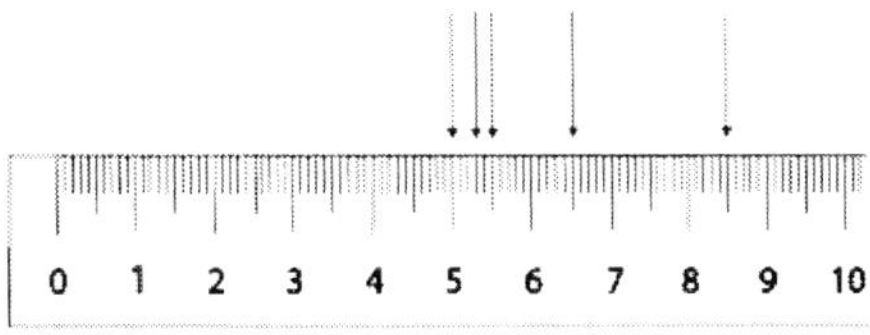

Here is a handy tool that might help you in your planning. I'm a visual learner — drawings and schematics really help me — so I like this tool. Take a ruler or tape measure and mark your age on it (or you can mark off the numbers on a piece of paper). In Sally's case she is 50, so we mark 50 mm. Also mark your life expectancy. Sally's life expectancy is 85. Kind of puts it all in perspective, eh? Do you have some other meaningful events that will happen in your life? Mark them off as well.

- Sally's St. Bernard dies: 53
- Sally sells her house and moves into an apartment: 55
- Sally's 13-year-old leaves home for university: 55
- Sally retires: 65
- Sally's grandchildren start university: 65

You can also make some educated guesses of things you can't accurately predict, like when you might transition from your fit phase of retirement to your contentment phase, your partner's retirement date if you have a partner, etc.

Now that you have some events marked down, does it put things into perspective for you?

Of course, these case studies are just scratching the surface, and only a qualified financial advisor can help with the financial fitness. Only a qualified fitness coach can assess your physical fitness. And only you know if you are emotionally ready for retirement. Talk with the people in your support group and get yourself Fit, Fit and Fit for your retirement.

One Year Later

My, how the time flies, especially when you're having a blast! Here it is, one year after my retirement and my wife and I discovered that we really were financially fit and physically fit enough to retire, and mainly emotionally fit, with a few adjustments. Let's take a look at our case study and see how things have unfolded.

Case Study #3 - Howard and Rosemary Pell

Background (as of January 2013):
Howard - 59, MSc Comp Sci, Trainer for the largest software company in Canada, no company pension.
Rosemary - 58, MBA, Independent Management Consultant for almost 20 years, no company pension.
No children, no St Bernard.

Life expectancy (based on Stats Canada):
Rosemary - 90 - as her family is quite long lived, we adjust her life expectancy to 95.
Howard - 85

Years until Howard retires at 60 = 1

Financial goal: to die with our last dollar in our pocket.

1. Financial Fitness:

Our financial advisors looked at our investments and agreed that we could both retire in 2014. However, in order to do so, we would have to accept that we don't have much of a buffer for emergencies, and we'd need to live a more frugal lifestyle, plus change our charitable giving from financial to more volunteering of our time. Our more frugal lifestyle has taken the form of fewer restaurant meals and more home-cooked meals, with more attention being paid to groceries that are on sale. We look for free or inexpensive entertainment rather than pricey concerts and plays. We also changed our vacation style: When I was travelling the world and amassing points from airlines, hotels and car rentals, we got used to taking rather lavish vacations with all those points. When I stopped travelling, those luxury vacations tapered off as we burned up our points. It took a while to accept that paying real money, rather than points, was really beyond our means. Today (and in the future), instead of business-class air, we're back in cattle-class; we've swapped JW Marriotts for B&Bs and apartment rentals; all-inclusive resorts in the Caribbean are replaced by a few days in a cottage at Wasaga Beach; and it is public transportation more often than renting a car (far easier to do in Europe than in Canada). And you know, I was always the driver, not that I minded, but now I too, get to sit back and enjoy the scenery.

I must admit that there have been a couple of surprises for my wife and me, things we didn't plan for or didn't plan well for. Insurance was a rude awakening for us. We didn't realize just how expensive it is or how little you get for your money. That is, if you want or need a lot of coverage, it can cost you a lot of money. We thought our teeth were in tip-top shape, but then, nearing the end of our first insurance year I needed an emergency root canal — I can't imagine agreeing to a root canal if it wasn't an emergency. Our insurance covered most of it — well, it would have covered most of it — but it seems I had used up most of my yearly allowance, and so $1,200 came out of our pockets. Then it turns out that our insurance plan doesn't cover crowns at all. Sixty-one years old and I've never had a crown; now that I need one, I don't have the insurance. But my dentist assured me that while he can't predict what will happen in every case, many people go without crowns for many, many years. Look Ma, no crown!

So we've taken the middle road on insurance. We didn't buy the most expensive and all-inclusive insurance, and we didn't opt to self-insure. Rather, we chose something in between, and so far it is working out not too badly. Even so, we are pretty much keeping to our planned goals, and at this rate there might even be a few bucks left over for our nieces and nephews when we both have no need for money.

Rose is still working, as she really enjoys her clients and her work, but as the dog days of the summer of 2015 remove the last chill of the winter of 2014/15 from our bones, she is spending a lot more time playing in the garden, golfing and relaxing in our garden with a gin and tonic. We're not sure when she'll formally retire, but when she does, we're financially fit for it.

2. Physical Fitness:

Both Rose and I have been regular gym rats for a few years. We started when I was working full time and diverted some money from our savings to our coach. When I joined the gym, I had no idea what

I was doing, so I hired a fitness coach. With all my raving about Coach Missy, Rose switched from her trainer to Missy too, and I was with Missy for about 2 years. We were both overjoyed for her family at the opportunity that took them away to Ottawa, but we were very sad to stop working with her. We have not hired another coach, but we do all our own programming from what we've learned from her over the years. Oh yes, she still encourages us via email and text, and we see her and her family once or twice a year.

I've talked about my own aches and pains, and I think you get the idea that I'm physically fit enough for my retirement. Rose also has her aches and pains, but she is also quite physically fit. This wasn't always the case. Some 15 years ago, a driver ran a stop sign in front of Rose, and other than writing off her Civic (she's never since found a car she enjoyed as much as that one), she was thankfully unhurt. However, she has been bothered by severe shoulder pain ever since. It really wasn't until she started with Missy, who took the time to understand Rose's limitations, that she started to feel less pain. That is, this injury had slowed her down for years and really held her back from doing the things she loves, like gardening, canoeing and kayaking as well as things she hates like shovelling snow. Now that she is in much less pain, I let her shovel all the snow she wants.

We still go to the gym 4 days a week or fewer if we are being very active; and aside from the limitations I've already talked about, we are quite fit for the kinds of things we want to do during our retirement.

3. Emotional Fitness:

I was so lucky that I could switch to part-time work for a year before I retired and really get a feel for: 1) living on less income and 2) living on more free time. It taught us a lot about what retirement was going to be like (or what it could be like if we wished), and so I was able to prepare myself emotionally.

One surprise, this one on the positive side, is just how busy I really am. Yes, people told me that they were busier now that they've retired, but I just laughed. I thought I'd have tons of time to laze about the backyard doing nothing but passive solar collection. Instead, my calendar is full, and I find that I have to say "no" quite a bit as opportunities keep coming my way. But seriously, I really can't imagine how I got things done when I was working 40 hours a week.

Of course, the biggest emotional transition has been from someone else depositing a pay cheque into our chequing account every 2 weeks, to our financial advisor moving **our** money from **our** investments into **our** chequing account. When I was working, whatever remained of my paycheque after paying the bills went into savings and investments. Now, we have our financial advisors transfer only what we think we'll need each month, and if we are a bit short we'll ask them to top it up. Shifting from **saving for** the future, to **spending in** our future, took a mental adjustment. While it really wasn't a surprise, it was and is quite difficult for both of us to get our monthly financial statement and see our savings decrease slightly. When I first retired, the market was still on an upswing, and even though we stopped making deposits, our balance was increasing. Then the markets took a turn, and we watched our savings decrease. Of course, our financial advisors had a plan that allowed us to wait out the storm and so, thanks to them, we are doing just fine. Sometimes, however, it is hard to remember that this is all part of the plan. The markets fluctuate, and with them, our savings. Even so, we are staying in the "okay zone" set by our financial advisors. We lived through 2008 and learned our lesson: Over time, the markets always increase, and we just need to wait out the bad times.

Case Closed

Six months after I retired, we took a two-week vacation at an adult-only, all-inclusive resort in Mexico (yes, it was planned). This is not the kind of vacation we normally do. We are normally found poking around museums, haunting art galleries and checking out architecture, but we were celebrating my retirement as well as my wife's 60th birthday so decided to go decadent for once. Lying on the beach isn't something we do well, even with a dozen trashy novels on our iPads and waiters walking by saying, "Margarita Meester?" One day, instead of reading on my iPad, I decided to write. And so the idea for this book arose. My thought was that retirement was going pretty well for us so far, and I wanted to share our success story with our friends. I thought I would just email a few pages to our friends, but as I wrote, I thought of more things I wanted to say, and you are now reading the closing lines of that book, started so many months ago on a beach in Mexico. Writing a book was probably the furthest thing from my mind when I retired, and yet, here it is. So no matter how much planning you do, you may find new opportunities that just can't be ignored.

Dan: Say Goodnight Dick.
Dick: Goodnight Dick.

It is time for you to take control of your life and get Fit, Fit and Fit. I can't help you any more than to encourage you to do the research now, before your retirement starts. Find a lawyer, a financial planner, a fitness coach, and possibly a life coach. Talk with your friends and family and, get recommendations. Check out the web for calculators and planning guides. Prepare yourself for this new phase of your life that we are so fortunate to have the opportunity to experience. If you have the luxury of a number of years before your retirement date, then you are in a great spot. If you're itching for retirement but not sure if you can, then start today to get more insight into the "how" and the "when."

Remember, the sooner you get Fit, Fit and Fit for retirement, the less stress you'll have, the easier the transition will be and the more rewarding your retirement years will be.

I wish you a long, healthy and Fit, Fit and Fit retirement.

Writing a book was an experience I'll never forget, self-publishing is something I wouldn't mind forgetting. I don't have a multi-million dollar marketing campaign, celebrity sponsors or an established network to sell through. If you found this book useful, please consider telling a friend, your financial advisor, your gym trainer, your life coach, a stranger walking his St. Bernard. If you have suggestions or ideas to help others prepare for their retirement, please consider sharing them on my blog at howardpell.ca.

Worksheets

Your Support Group

Add to this list as you like and then check them off the list as you speak with them.

- ☐ Financial advisor
  - What do I need to do before I retire?
  - When is the earliest date I can retire?
- ☐ Lawyer
  - Are all my documents in order?
- ☐ Accountant
  - Are all my documents in order?
  - What steps, if any, should I take before retirement to benefit my tax situation in retirement?
- ☐ Fitness coach
  - Am I on track to achieving my physical fitness?
- ☐ Doctor
  - Are there any medical reasons to retire early, or later?
  - Are there alternatives to the high-priced drugs I am taking that my new insurance may not cover?
  - Are there medical procedures I could do now that my new insurance may not cover?
- ☐ Dentist
  - Are there dental issues I could do now that my new insurance may not cover?
- ☐ Your direct manager, and if appropriate, your manager's manager
  - When is the earliest date I can retire?

- ☐ The rest of your family, your children, siblings and parents if they are still alive
  - Are there any family issues that we need to address before I retire? During my retirement?

Time Line

Develop the time line starting today and working towards your retirement date, or choose your retirement date and work backwards to today. Either way, you want to include all the various events that need to occur between these two dates.

Start Today

Make appointments with everyone in your support group, and prepare a list of questions for each of them. Meeting with everyone could take weeks or even months to arrange, so don't be in too much of a hurry. As you speak to each support person, mark their estimate of your retirement date on your time line. Again, this could amount to weeks, months or even years. For example, do you have a great dental plan with your company, and do your teeth need some work? Do you still have mercury fillings? Now's the time to have them replaced with porcelain (or whatever the latest is) while your company's insurance will pay for it. That could take months if your dentist is really busy.

Next, we'll go back to the list of your Pre-Retirement expenses you made. Put all those items in your time line. Let's also add the various other events that you identified, like the kid's university graduation present, the kid's weddings etc.

Your Time Line

If you're handy with spreadsheets, you can whip one up showing dates, tasks (to be done and completed) and who you're waiting for to complete the tasks. Then it is really easy to move things around as dates change. If you don't like computers or spreadsheets, then perhaps recipe cards or slips of paper and a cork board will work better for you. In either case, a visual display of where you are and where you're going is really nice, and it helps to keep you on track.

Item / Task	Who	Earliest Retirement Date	Completed
Financial fitness attained	Financial Advisor(s)		
Physical fitness attained	Personal Trainer, Sports Coach, Exercise Leader		
Emotional fitness attained	Life coach, partner, family, etc.		
Will(s), POA(s), executor, etc.	Lawyer	N/A	
Tax planning, etc.	Accountant		
Medical	Doctor		
Dental	Dentist		
Eyes	Optometrist		
Give notice at work	Your manager(s)		
New roof	Roofer		
Anniversary trip to Mexico	Partner		
St. Bernard Puppy	Vet and breeder		

Appendix A

Appendix A

The 3-Fitness Plan for Retirement: Worksheet

You've read the book; you've reflected on the questions; now, it's time for you to create your 3-Fitness Plan for Retirement. Photocopy the next few pages and record your thoughts about your Retirement journey. Use this as a discussion guide with your financial advisor; with your fitness/health coaches and with your emotional support team, to create a plan to give meaning and opportunity for your retirement years.

Here is a guide to using the worksheets:

Financially Fit:

1. Record your current income from all sources.
2. Identify the expenses you currently have that you won't need or could eliminate/reduce when you retire (e.g. no more commuting expenses; or the daily "double double" on the way to work; or the RRSP savings currently set aside from your annual income)
3. Estimate expenses you will need in retirement that you don't have now (e.g. 6 weeks in Spain in the winter; private health insurance premiums and costs; monthly trips to see the grandkids; dance lessons; vet bills for the St. Bernard puppy you plan to adopt)
4. Net it out – will your expenses go up or down? Deduct – or add – the difference from your current income. If nothing else changes, this is a ball-park starting point for your retirement income.
5. Can your current savings and pension estimates support this ball-park income, with inflation and taxes for the remainder of your life? If not, seek advice and start planning your actions now to close the revenue & expenses gap, either before or shortly after retirement.

Physically Fit:

1. Record your current fitness markers – weight; BMI; capacity; health issues or limitations. Can you play sports? Can you run? How about easily climbing stairs without suffering?
2. Identify your fitness goals based on your image of a "good retirement" (e.g. do you hope to start, or continue, dancing or hiking or playing ball with your grandkids? Do you want to continue living in your home and play in the garden for hours a day to produce a prize-winning rose? How about those daily walks with your St. Bernard?)
3. What health limitations exist that you need to take note of now, that might hamper your goals? Start working on managing those issues today – it's never too early. Plus, if you have good company health benefit coverage, now is the time for the expenses of physiotherapy or chiropractic treatments to straighten you out and resolve your tendinitis, or start the dental treatments that you've delayed.

Emotionally Fit:

1. Identify what you *currently* do to give yourself a sense of purpose and to create social and intellectual fulfillment (e.g. book club; look after the grandkids; volunteer; cycling group). If the dominant item on your list is "my current work", ask yourself – do you intend to continue to do that in your 70's? 80's? For a few of you, yes, you probably can and will. For most – it is unlikely.
2. Identify what you *would like to do* in retirement to give meaning to your life (e.g. read all those books set aside for years; start cooking meals again; learn to play a musical instrument; keep dancing)
3. Identify if there are any physical or financial barriers to this "would like to do" list. Create a plan to close the gap or to modify your wishes.

4. If your "would like to do" list was very short or your answer was "I'm not sure", return to the Emotional Fitness chapter to start to identify interests you held at one time and would like to do again; or determine what skills and interests you have in your work and life today that you want to keep using. This will start you on the path of determining how to fan those embers of interest into flames of purpose.

Ready? Time to get started and pull it all together!

Financially Fit: Preliminary Worksheet

A starting point for discussions with your financial advisor

Step I: Identify Pre-Retirement Income

Current Annual After-Tax Income = (1)	$

Step II: Estimate the Change in Net-After Tax Income Requirements:

(Current expenses such as work-related costs, RRSP contributions, and "one-time" purchases such as house renovations will be reduced or eliminated, while costs related to activities in retirement years will be added):

Annual Expenses, Not Needed While Retired		New Annual Expenses While Retired	
(e.g. commuting expenses)	$	*(e.g. Private health insurance)*	$
	$		$
	$		$
	$		$
	$		$
	$		$
	$		$
Total (A):	$	Total (B):	$

Decrease/(Increase) in Post-Retirement Expenses (Subtract A – B) = (2)	$

Ball-park Income Needed After Expense Changes (Subtract 1 – 2) = (3)	$

Step III: Estimate Annual Income Sources in Retirement

(Pensions and withdrawals from your savings will be the main sources of your retirement income)

Annual Government Pensions	$
Annual Company Pension (if any)	$
Annual Withdrawal from Investment/Savings, as Planned	$
Other:	$
Other:	$
Total Annual Retirement Income Expected = (C)	$

Retirement Income Required from Other Sources: (Subtract C – 3) = (4)	$
If (4) is a positive number = Hooray! *Your projected income is greater than your expected ball-park needs.*	
If (4) is a negative number = Yipes! *You have some steps to take to close the gap ... proceed to Step IV.*	

Financially Fit: Preliminary Worksheet, continued

Step IV: Closing the Gap Between "Have" and Need"

A "negative number" happens if retirement income sources (4) are less than the ball-park income needed (3)

Withdraw Extra from Capital/Savings		Yes: ❑		No: ❑
	If yes, amount/yr:			
Reduce Expenses		Yes: ❑		No: ❑
	If yes, amount/yr:			
Work part-time		Yes: ❑		No: ❑
	If yes, amount/yr:			
Retire later		Yes: ❑		No: ❑
	If yes, how long:			
Other sources or actions?				

Questions to Discuss with Financial Advisor to Become Financially Fit:

Physically Fit: Preliminary Worksheet

A starting point for discussions with your physical fitness team

Item A - Current Fitness Snapshot:

Age		Height		Date	
Weight		B.M.I.		Blood Pressure	

Give an honest assessment of your:	*Great*	*Good*	*OK*	*Varies*	*Poor*
1. Overall health	❑	❑	❑	❑	❑
2. Body strength	❑	❑	❑	❑	❑
3. Flexibility	❑	❑	❑	❑	❑
4. Pain levels	❑	❑	❑	❑	❑
5. Endurance /Cardio	❑	❑	❑	❑	❑
6. Balance	❑	❑	❑	❑	❑
7. Nutritional Habits	❑	❑	❑	❑	❑

Based on your activity goals, how important is it to have good:	*Essential*	*Quite Relevant*	*Not Sure*	*Low Relevance*	*Not Relevant*
1. Overall health	❑	❑	❑	❑	❑
2. Body strength	❑	❑	❑	❑	❑
3. Flexibility	❑	❑	❑	❑	❑
4. Pain levels	❑	❑	❑	❑	❑
5. Endurance /Cardio	❑	❑	❑	❑	❑
6. Balance	❑	❑	❑	❑	❑
7. Nutritional Habits	❑	❑	❑	❑	❑

Item B - Fitness Impact on Retirement Activity Goals:
Identify those items where your current state of physical fitness is not high enough to match its importance for your activity goals. What barrier are you facing? *(e.g. you want to do more gardening, but your flexibility for bending is poor; you'd like to hike the West Coast Trail but you have painful knees and low cardio endurance)*

Activity I want to do:	Requires I'm able to:	Current physical barrier:

Physically Fit: Preliminary Worksheet, continued

Item C – Priorities to Build Physical Fitness Levels:

Which items create the highest barriers to your goal, and should be your highest priority for action?	*Immediate Priority*	*High Priority*	*Improve Later*	*Lower Priority*	*Maintain*
1. Overall health	❏	❏	❏	❏	❏
2. Body strength	❏	❏	❏	❏	❏
3. Flexibility	❏	❏	❏	❏	❏
4. Pain levels	❏	❏	❏	❏	❏
5. Endurance /Cardio	❏	❏	❏	❏	❏
6. Balance	❏	❏	❏	❏	❏
7. Nutritional Habits	❏	❏	❏	❏	❏

Immediate Actions for Immediate Priorities:

Item D – Areas to Address While Receiving Company Health Benefits:

(e.g. dental improvements, new glasses)

Questions to Discuss with Your Team to Become Physically Fit:

Emotionally Fit: Preliminary Worksheet

A starting point for discussions with your support team

Part A: Your Emotional Support Team

You will be making many changes in your daily life and focus, and will benefit from the encouragement of others. Who are the main people in your life you can turn to for support, inspiration and insights?

•	•
•	•
•	•

Part B: Current Involvements Outside of Your Work Life

What primary activities, hobbies, or involvements do you currently have outside of your work? Which do you hope to continue/do more of once you retire? Which are you ready to do less of, or stop altogether? *(e.g. gardening, sports, volunteering, choir, dining with friends, reading...)*

Fulfilling Activities Outside of Work:	*Hope to ......*
	Do More Continue Do Less
	Do More Continue Do Less
	Do More Continue Do Less
	Do More Continue Do Less
	Do More Continue Do Less

Part C: Giving Meaning to Your Life in Retirement – What do you Want to Do?

With your new-found freedom from work schedules, deadlines, and expectations, what would you want to do with your time and energy?

Activities & Involvement For My Emotional Fitness	*Are You Financially and Physically Fit For It*		
	Yes!	Almost	Not Really
	Yes!	Almost	Not Really
	Yes!	Almost	Not Really
	Yes!	Almost	Not Really
	Yes!	Almost	Not Really

Where you didn't circle the "Yes!" Option, return to your Financially & Physically Fit worksheets to make plans to get ready. Or, do a reality check to determine if your "want" list needs to be modified.

If you struggled to create this list, move to Part D to reflect on what inspires you.

Emotionally Fit: Preliminary Worksheet - continued

Part D: What Gives You Fulfillment Now?
Rather than trying to define "what" you want to do, try reflecting on those features of your life that currently, or in the past, provide satisfaction and fulfillment.

When you retire from your work, there may be features of the work or workplace that you will miss. Perhaps it is the social side of being in a team; or the challenge of solving difficult questions; or the prestige of being part of something important. Also, what talents or skills do you want to keep using? Determine what motivates you now, and use that as a base to identify activities that could create the same positive impact for your life after you leave the employment world.

What do you love about your work – what will you miss about being at work?	*What might you do to replace that benefit?*

Similarly, what type of activities did you enjoy doing in your past, which you set aside before life, family, work, and other responsibilities claimed your time.

I used to enjoy	*Do I want to re-focus my time to do this now?*		
	Yes!	Maybe	Unlikely
	Yes!	Maybe	Unlikely
	Yes!	Maybe	Unlikely
	Yes!	Maybe	Unlikely
	Yes!	Maybe	Unlikely

Are you Financially and Physically Fit enough to pursue the "Yes!" activities or to investigate the "Maybe" ones? If not, consider how you might adjust either your goals or one of your Fitness plans.

Emotionally Fit: Preliminary Worksheet - continued

Part E: Are there any Big "1-Time" changes you Expect to Do?
Sometimes we put off a big decision or activity until we have more time, so we wait until retirement to get started. Make note of these now, but remember that those activities will likely keep you focused only for the short-term so start also developing your "want to do."

Have you been waiting for more time before you: renovate/ downsize? trade your SUV for a sports car? change your relationship? Plan for these now, to note both the financial and emotional impact

The "One-Time"/ "Have More Time" Activities	*Financial Impact? Time/ Energy Impact?*